THE JOURNEY to COVENTRY
Tortured but not Defeated

Lois T.A. Omorayewa

authorHOUSE

AuthorHouse™ UK
1663 Liberty Drive
Bloomington, IN 47403 USA
www.authorhouse.co.uk
Phone: 0800 047 8203 (Domestic TFN)
+44 1908 723714 (International)

© 2019 Lois T.A. Omorayewa. All rights reserved.

No part of this book may be reproduced, stored in a retrieval system, or transmitted by any means without the written permission of the author.

Scripture taken from the New King James Version®. Copyright © 1982 by Thomas Nelson. Used by permission. All rights reserved.

Published by AuthorHouse 06/19/2019

ISBN: 978-1-7283-8917-2 (sc)
ISBN: 978-1-7283-8916-5 (e)

Print information available on the last page.

Any people depicted in stock imagery provided by Getty Images are models, and such images are being used for illustrative purposes only. Certain stock imagery © Getty Images.

This book is printed on acid-free paper.

Because of the dynamic nature of the Internet, any web addresses or links contained in this book may have changed since publication and may no longer be valid. The views expressed in this work are solely those of the author and do not necessarily reflect the views of the publisher, and the publisher hereby disclaims any responsibility for them.

To God Almighty, who has continuously seen me through life since the minute I was born. Also, I am honoured, grateful, humbled, and thankful for this great opportunity. Thank you for choosing me to implement this project.

To anyone who has experienced or is currently experiencing any mental health challenges, this one is for you. You are strong, you are important, and you matter. The world needs you, and you will pull through.

Acknowledgements

I can't thank God enough for the amazing people he has put in my life and the ones he has connected me to.

To my family, my dad, my mum, and my baby brother, King, I can't thank you enough for standing by me, even when you didn't understand things. Thank you for everything you did and continue to do. Thank you for praying for and with me. Thank you for encouraging me, thank you for collecting my prescriptions, and thank you for going to buy whatever I was craving, even when it wasn't exactly convenient for you. Thank you for always telling me I was healed, even when it didn't look like it. This is not just my but our testimony. May affliction never arise again; I love you guys!

To my grandmother, Iya Taiyelolu, who took it upon herself to pray for me relentlessly. Thank you for all the love and support, even from a distance. May your labour of love on all of us never be in vain.

To Bishop Abioye, thank you, sir, for agreeing with me in prayer. Thank you for reinforcing the importance of speaking in tongues with me. You told me to always keep saying "Thank you, Jesus"—even in situations that I didn't understand. I can't wait to see you soon and discuss this testimony with you face-to-face.

To my counsellor, Juli-Ann, wow, where do I start? You have seen me both weak and strong, you have seen me lying in bed and sitting up, you have seen me cry and laugh, you have seen me sad and happy, you have seen me encouraged and discouraged, you have seen me angry and calm, you have seen me lose and gain weight, and so on. Thank you for your patience, love, and support. Thinking of our journey together so far from that very first session when I felt I was not looking presentable until how far we have worked well together by his grace makes me want to cry tears of joy. Thank you, Juli-Ann, for everything.

To Dr David Craft, Juli-Ann and I prayed for direction and found you. We had only three sessions, during which you helped me calm down and relax at my own pace. As skinny as I looked in reality, you looked at my graduation picture and told me I could go back to that healthy-looking person. You told me I could go to church and work again. You told me I didn't have agoraphobia. You told me I could eat anything I wanted. You made me visualise throwing away the baggage of fear, anxiety, phobias, and an eating disorder and replacing it with fruits of courage, boldness, healing, restoration, and peace, helping me carry them visually everywhere I went. You took my very first walk since the "eating disorder" incident with me. You are amazing!

Dr Chris and Dr Ronke Olukanni, where do I begin to thank you? For the unplanned visits, for the phone consultations after you had a long day at work, for your love and support, I say thank you. You both had so much faith that I was going to be OK. You always made yourself available. There was a point where Auntie Ronke and I were talking on the phone after work nearly every day; after talking about my eating habits, we would talk about many other things and laugh. She was never in a hurry to go. Dr Chris, you told me many times that I am a winner to the point that I started saying it to myself subconsciously. You both encouraged and prayed for me. Thank you so much. May you never have a reason to weep over any of your children.

To one of my other mums, Dr Titi Oshoba, thank you for everything, for the recommendations, for the resources, for the Bible scriptures, for the bedtime and wake-up affirmations, for praying with me, and for the phone calls and text messages.

To my pastors in Nigeria, Pastor Sam and Pastor Isaac, you walked through this journey with me from a distance. Sirs, you both were sure that all was going to be well, even when I was on the verge of giving up. Thank you so much, sirs. I can't thank you enough for everything.

To my Pastor in London, Pastor B, Resident daddy, Resident mummy, and my finance department family, especially Auntie Tara, Minister Tunde, and my entire Glory House family, thank you so much for all your love and support.

To my amazing best friend, my sister, my gist partner, my future maid of honour, and the future God-mother to my future children, Vanessa, thank you for always being there, coming with me to GP appointments, getting some of my prescriptions, and always helping me out and being there. I will never forget the day you reminded me about how when God wanted to elevate Joseph in the Bible and use him, he allowed him to be put in a well and eventually sold as a slave. Cheers to many more years of friendship.

To Imran, thank you for always being there even though you are far away. To Salim, Awati, Somto, Abiola, Becky, Bisola, Sharon, and all the lovely people I met in Coventry, thank you for everything.

To all my friends and well-wishers—those who visited and/or called, messaged, and so on (I would rather not list names here to avoid missing out on any)—thank you so much.

To my line manager at work, Andreas, to Graham, my entire team, and the organisation at large, thank you for being understanding and supportive. Thank you for still trusting in my abilities and allowing me to remain a part of you.

Finally, to you, my reader, thank you for giving me a chance to tell you my story and inspire you. I hope you enjoy the book, and I pray that God will give you the grace and strength to challenge and defeat whatever challenges you. Enjoy!

Introduction

The Assignment

Growing up, I wrote short stories and always wanted to be an author of at least one book. However, I never took it seriously and grew out of it, but little did I know that God had other plans. I am writing this book because God laid it upon my heart to do so and it sounded easier accepting the instruction than actually doing it. The first time the title of this book dropped upon my heart was on Wednesday, 26 April 2018, and I wrote a note on my phone: "The Journey to Coventry—Smiling Externally but Anxious Internally. Although I wrote it down, I never did anything about it. I had been going through health challenges, which in one word was *anxiety*.

I started to feel less like my real self, as it affected almost every area of my life. It did not feel normal; I don't know how to explain it, but I kept having the feeling that there was more to everything that was going on. Life felt difficult enough, as did praying, but I added a new prayer request: "Lord, there is more to this. What do you want me to learn from all this? Holy Spirit, please speak to me". Believe me when I say that this was a difficult prayer to pray. Sometimes

I felt I did not even have the physical or spiritual strength to pray because of how low I felt. Furthermore, I wanted to be sure I meant the prayer and heard from God, making sure I was not making things up in my head. I remember my mum saying to me a few times that maybe God wanted to draw me closer to himself, but I would think, *Not really.* I knew I had a good relationship with God, and if anything, I was scared that season of my life was trying to tamper with my relationship with God, but it all adds up now because I am more passionate about God than I have ever been. I have also learned that we can't have enough of God. There is always *more*.

Finally, he spoke! God spoke! It was during the early hours of 20 January 2019, at about 2 a.m. Earlier on, I had tried to nap (but couldn't) and set my alarm for 11.50 p.m. so I could wish my dad a happy birthday at exactly 12 a.m. That happened, and we ended up chatting away. When I left my parents' room to go back to my room, I was so tired and decided to lie down for ten minutes before getting ready for bed; within a few minutes, I heard God so clearly that it was both shocking and exciting at the time, as all that was on my mind at the time was sleep.

The assignment, which I have titled "The God's Project", entails three aspects in no particular order: this book, the birth of a foundation to promote mental health awareness (specifically anxiety and depression) in Nigeria; The Bring It Home Foundation (BIH), and a YouTube channel to help people suffering with mental health challenges in the little way I can, using my own experience. This was a big deal for me, especially the YouTube channel, which is naturally not my thing. I was about to go from barely ever having a display picture on WhatsApp to telling the world my story, but bring it on because "I [Lois] can do all things through Christ Jesus that strengths me" (Phil. 4:13 NKJV). I started praying about it all, and this time praying got easier and more exciting.

My career is along the lines of a junior project manager, so I am privileged to also be managing a project for God. I pray that this book blesses you as you read it and that God's will alone for this book is fulfilled.

Disclaimer

Before I proceed, I should clearly state that I am not a mental health expert at all. In fact, it took my experience for me to understand truly the depth of mental health, and sometimes I still don't fully get it. Therefore, this book is mostly based on my experience. Another disclaimer I would like to give is that you will come across God a whole lot in this book. However, this book is not directed at a specific religion. It is written with the intention for anyone to be able to read it and feel inspired that mental health challenges do not equal the end of the world. Yes, I am born again and was born into a Christian family, but I have grown to find my purpose in Christ, independent of what family I was born into or how I was raised.

Different people have different coping mechanisms, but for me, during what felt like the most difficult season in my life, when I think about it, the only way I can explain it is that God literally walked with me through fire. I am an emotional and sensitive person, and for that alone, I know I could have only pulled through because of God. Everything I went through felt horrible at the time, but somehow, with the help of God, I always pulled through and overcame. I often had to work my faith, but I still can't take the credit, for even the ability to work my faith was yet again by the grace of the Almighty God—it's deep. This same God in Galatians 5:14 has said that we should love our neighbours as ourselves. He also said in Galatians 6:2 that we should "bear one another's burdens and so fulfil the law of Christ" (NKJV), so it makes sense that he does not want me to keep all of these experiences to myself, right?

Chapter 1
HOW IT ALL BEGAN

The 2017 Lois before Coventry

The 2017 Lois before Coventry was a reserved but bubbly and active young woman. She was full of life, liked to dress up, go out, eat, and so on. She seldom used to fall ill; all she ever had when down was a cold, headache, or occasionally a sore throat. This Lois had not needed to visit a doctor for eight years. In July 2017, she turned 21 years old and graduated with a BSc in Computer Science with Business Management. Over the past year, she developed an interest in project management and decided to pursue a master's degree in Programme and Project Management at the University of Warwick in Coventry, and that's where everything started to change within a month of arriving at Coventry.

The Beginning of the Journey

Prior to the incident that led to dealing with anxiety, I never felt sick or nauseated. Sometimes I got curious when people complained of the various symptoms, as I literally didn't know how they felt. In the department I was in at Warwick, we completed a module in a week. It was extremely intensive, from Monday through Friday, from 9 a.m. until 6.30 p.m. (there were times we left as late as 7 or even 8). This particular week, it was just my second module; it was a stressful one because many people were ill with a cold, so there was constant coughing and sneezing through the week.

By Thursday, I had picked up a cold too, which was exhausting, but I thought to myself that at least tomorrow was Friday and the module would end. Fast-forward to Saturday later that week ... I felt off, but I did not know what it was and did not make much of it, just carrying on with my day. The same thing happened on Sunday, but I was still able to go to church, cook, and even eat well through the day. That evening, I even took a walk and then got ice cream because I was so bored and had not really made friends yet in my accommodation.

However, later that night, I was having my nightly shower in preparation for bed when my stomach started to feel tight. It was weird, as I could never remember having any stomach issues before that point. I rushed my shower to lie in bed. It subsided a bit, and I fell asleep.

The following day, Monday, I got up early as usual. Although I did not have lectures that week, I still preferred to go into the university from morning to evening, as I preferred working in the library. This feeling off was still there, but again, I was not making much of it. I was in the library by 9.30 a.m. but was only able to work comfortably for an

The Journey to Coventry

hour before I started to feel restless and uncomfortable. I kept wondering if I was tired or what. I stayed there for a while, but there was no form of productivity, so I decided to take a walk; maybe I just needed a bit of fresh air, I thought, then I would be back.

A few steps outside, I started to feel a strong and overwhelming sensation from my legs upwards. It was nausea. Wow, what was going on? I forgot what nausea felt like, as I was about twelve or thirteen the last time I was ill, aside from having a cold. I managed to get myself back to my accommodation.

Fast-forward to Wednesday ... I knew I could not continue like this. At this point, I had lost my appetite and was quickly becoming weak. I then decided to go to a walk-in clinic, as I had only registered with a GP two days earlier online on the Monday that the incident happened, and I was unsure if I was already fully registered. Please don't make the same mistake I made; irrespective of how healthy you are, always ensure you are registered with a GP. The stress that day was beyond me. I left in the morning just after 9 a.m. and did not get back until just before 7 p.m. I was all by myself. After waiting for hours in the walk-in centre, I was referred to another hospital because the walk-in centre could not find what was wrong. It was at the second hospital that I was then diagnosed with gastroenteritis—the stomach bug. That was the first time I had heard about such a thing.

The stomach bug, although a horrible experience, is usually perceived as not being a big deal and is expected to go away within a few days. The only medication I was given was antisickness Cyclizine to deal with nausea, but nothing for the bug, as I was told it is a virus and is usually left to run its course. However, for me, this was the beginning of real pain. From that period in October 2017 until I went back home in London for Christmas, I was pretty much unwell. I had lost my appetite, and all I had was toast, melon and grapes fruit pots, bananas, corn, ginger tea, Lucozade, and water.

Thankfully, the amazing people I had met in my accommodation (who are now my good friends) were aware of what was going on and showed so much love and support when they barely knew me (Salim, Awati, Somto, Abiola, Becky, and Bisola, I can never forget you guys). They played different roles such as helping me get my groceries, prescriptions, going to hospital appointments with me, and coming to check up on me and spend time with me. One good thing that came out of it all is we became one big family. I saw Awati and Salim every day. We studied together, relaxed together, cooked together, and made noise together, of course.

Back to the week of the stomach bug ... By Sunday, I felt a little better. However, I woke up in the middle of the night feeling weird, and my body felt heavy. I was dizzy; it's amazing how sometimes your body has a way of communicating to you. I had never truly felt dizzy before. I think I just opened the window, said a word of prayer, and went back to sleep. The next morning, I woke up and as I got up, I couldn't see. My room was spinning, and it felt as if I were swimming, so I quickly went to open my room door just in case anything happened. Upon lying back down, I called the ambulance and one of my friends, as the rest had gone for lectures. I later found out that my friend ran

The Journey to Coventry

from his room on the seventh floor to reception without any footwear to inform them of what had happened. The care my now-friends showed me, who at the time barely knew me, is amazing. Now, even more than ever, I want to always help people where possible, no matter how little. The Bible says in Philippians 2:4, "Let each of you look out not only for his own interests, but also for the interests of others" (NKJV). My beloved reader, I want you to pause for a moment and think, do you really help people? If you help people, do you always expect something in return? ("It is more blessed to give than to receive" [Acts 20:35 NKJV].) I am encouraging everyone including myself to make a conscious decision and effort to start helping people more and showing them that you care. It is not too much to put a smile on one person's face daily, even if it is by a simple word of encouragement or affirmation.

The ambulance arrived, and after doing some checks, they didn't see anything wrong and therefore were not going to take me to the hospital as I had expected. When I insisted, they said if they took me to the hospital, I could be waiting for up to ten hours because I was not in danger and because I was young and usually fit and healthy. I wouldn't be considered an emergency. Oh, dear England!

It took my dad calling a family friend who was a doctor, and he said the issue was vertigo (dizziness with a spinning sensation). Again, I had never heard of vertigo. The doctor called me and told me what to request from my doctor in Coventry, which I did (Dr Chris, thank you for always making yourself available, as busy as you are). That day, my amazing best friend, Vanessa, left everything she was doing unplanned and travelled from her university in

Leicester to Coventry to come and look after me. I felt much better in the night and was able to have a fruit pot, as I had not eaten anything the entire day.

At the beginning of this book, I said God walked with me through fire. My master's course had no exams and was assessed based on coursework and a dissertation. I was working on my first coursework when the library situation happened (in total, I was to complete ten coursework over the year). I often had to work on my first coursework in bed. However, as God would have it, when I got my first distinction on my first coursework, I was shocked. Then there was the second coursework to do for my second module, which ended the week before the stomach bug. I literally had to complete this one in bed, as I still was not feeling too well. At this point, my appetite was poor.

The deadline for the second coursework was towards the end of November 2017. The day I finished the coursework, I decided to give myself a break, try to get something to eat, and then proofread one more time and submit. I decided to order Nando's using Deliveroo. When the Deliveroo driver arrived, I dreaded going downstairs because I was tired. I had been working on my coursework and had not been eating, which was enough to make me weak. However, I went anyway. I got into the lift. On getting to the ground floor, out of the lift, and walking towards reception, I started to feel funny. I didn't know what it was, but the more I walked, the more something felt off. By the time I got to the Deliveroo driver, I was leaning on the wall. I managed to collect my order and then decided to sit in the reception area for a bit. The receptionist on duty looked at me and asked if I was OK. I said I was fine.

After about five or ten minutes, I managed to stand up and asked the receptionist for help with getting back upstairs, as I had no clue what was going on. The receptionist agreed to help, and as we approached the lift, I had an overwhelming sensation through my body and a wave of nausea. I still don't really know how to explain how I felt in that moment. I just remember saying that I needed to sit down, and I walked right back to the reception area. At this point, I was gasping for air and breathing through my mouth. The receptionist followed me and asked, "Are you going to be sick?" I said yes. He said, "Right. Calm down. Do you want some water?"

I said, "No, thank you. I'll be fine. I just need to sit here for a bit."

At this point, I feared going into the lift, and there was no way I was going to go into it that night, alone or with people. I brought out my phone to call one of my friends, and while doing that, fortunately one of my other friends whose room was directly opposite mine was just coming in from lectures. My two friends helped me up the stairs from the ground floor to the second floor where my room was. It was traumatic and exhausting. As soon as I got to my room, I immediately went to lie down on my bed. I was instantly relieved. However, I felt weird in the sense that all I could think of for the following few minutes was, *What just happened?* Something in me said it was a panic attack—not that I really understood a panic attack before that point. I can't remember what I googled, but from all indications, I had just had a panic attack, which was also confirmed by my doctor a few days later.

This was the first of quite a few panic attacks and anxiety-related symptoms. I became scared of having another panic attack. I did not have the strength to cook, but even when I was ordering my usual groceries or mashed potatoes from Nando's, I would make sure one of my friends was available to go downstairs and help me pick it up. I was due to go home to London on 15 December 2017. This was only about two and a half weeks away from the first panic attack. However, another worry set in. I was not strong enough because I was consuming way below four hundred calories daily, and now I had experienced a panic attack from just going downstairs, so how was I supposed to get to London? Coventry to London Euston was one journey, but getting home from London Euston was another long and not-so-pleasant journey on its own, especially during rush hour.

I started overthinking about getting home safely. In this season of my life, I had come to understand how powerful the mind is and how it can affect our lives, both positively and negatively, depending on how we use it and what we entertain in it. Recently I had been able to understand Jeremiah 29:11 from different angles. God said, "For I know the thoughts that I think towards you ... the thought of peace and not of evil, to give you a future and a hope" (NKJV). When I meditated on it, I thought that even God, who is the creator of heaven and earth, acknowledges the importance of thinking. He could have easily said he would give us peace and a future and that would still be fantastic, but it felt special knowing he was thinking and planning these things and now making us aware. It's just like saying, "Child, don't worry. I have you!" Another Bible version of the same scripture says, "For I know the plans I have for you", but when we plan, we think, right?

The Journey to Coventry

Eventually, I asked my brother, who attended university in Nottingham, to come to Coventry on 14 December 2017 since we were both scheduled to go back to London the following day. However, I started worrying again about how I would get home. Eventually, I called my dad and asked if he could come and pick up my brother and I from Coventry on Friday, to which he made himself available. I again started worrying and stressing over the journey. I was wondering if I would be OK in the car for a two-hour journey, as I had not been outside for nearly two and a half weeks. A few days before I was due to leave Coventry, I got my friend to help me buy travel sickness tablets. I didn't have travel sickness and had never experienced it, but I just felt the need to have them to keep me calm because although I really wanted to be out of there, I was worrying over the process of getting home.

On the evening of 13 December 2017, I asked my friend to take a small walk with me downstairs (I knew my brother was coming the next day, and I was hoping to go downstairs to let him in). As we were going down the stairs, it didn't feel that bad—until it was time to come back to the second floor. As we were coming back up, it was OK initially. I think it was about four flights, but the more we climbed, the more I started to feel weaker and weaker, to the point that my heart started racing and I rushed to lie down in bed. I felt relieved, again wondering what just happened. Was it another panic attack? Up until then, I didn't know. I immediately reminded my friend that my brother was coming the next day and asked to help bring him up when he arrived.

When my brother arrived the next day, oh, the joy in my heart to see him at last. However, I felt so bad that I could not be the one to bring him upstairs. I ordered him food, which he had to go pick up downstairs by himself, but he understood, as always. When I experienced the first panic attack, I had told one of my friends that after a couple of days, we should be taking frequent walks. However, each time taking a walk was raised, I always had an excuse to not go out because of fear of the unknown.

When it was time to leave, I was anxious about the journey but excited to go home finally. When my dad arrived, he called us to come downstairs, as he had encountered a lot of traffic driving to Coventry and wanted us to leave as soon as possible in order to prevent being stuck in traffic again. I told my brother to take both of our suitcases to the car. When he finally returned, it was now time for us to both go downstairs. I could feel the uneasiness kicking in. As we stepped out of my room, I said I needed to sit down and went back into the room to sit down for a minute or two. My brother kept asking if I was OK. I knew I had to go, so I braced myself and we left the room again. I had already told my brother that we were going to use the stairs due to the lift incident. As we approached the stairs, I started going down weirdly, my neck tilted. I was shaking and gasping for air.

As soon as we got to the ground floor, my body calmed down and these symptoms eased off. My brother was traumatized about the situation because, according to him, he had never seen me that way. In the car, I didn't talk much and didn't move much. I stayed in the same position the entire journey. I was listening to music and holding my

The Journey to Coventry

Bible to my stomach to feel calm. I tried forcing myself to sleep through the journey, but I couldn't even sleep for one minute. There was a lot of traffic, and I kept checking the time and occasionally using the map app on my phone to check how long it would take to get home. I just wanted to be home. I think it's safe to say my family were shocked. Although they knew I had not been feeling 100 per cent, they did not know the gravity, as I tried to talk normally with them whenever we were on the phone. I had lost a lot of weight and was lethargic.

Looking back at the initial challenge, I should have handled my thought patterns better, but thank God for growth. I cannot tell you how much I had noticed how my thought patterns shaped my day, my mood, how I felt, what I said, the decisions I made, and so on. I personally feel we all need to start paying attention and putting much more effort towards our thought patterns. If you already have a good and positive thought pattern, that's fantastic, but it still requires hard work to be maintained and to get better. Let's be realistic: no matter how much we pray and try to stay strong, life is full of challenges, but as long as we play our part, God has our backs: "These things I have spoken to you, that in me you may have peace. In the world you will have tribulation; but be of good cheer, I have overcome the world" (John 16:33 NKJV).

The first few days being home were not exactly easy in terms of how I was still feeling, but being back home with my family for a while meant a lot. Although I started to eat a little better than in Coventry, my strength levels were not so great. I remember always being in my room and hardly ever coming downstairs. Going to church was not easy, but

I pulled through. I remember receiving so many questions and comments about my weight, such as, "What happened to you?", "You have lost a lot of weight", and "What is your diet plan?"

To cut the long story short, after visiting the GP and having blood tests, I started taking vitamins and I was eating gradually; I started to get a better in time for Christmas. On Christmas Day, although I looked quite tiny due to the weight loss, I was happy and full of life. I dressed up and wore make-up. It had been a long since I had done all of this, and I was so full of life due to everything that had been going on for the last couple of weeks. For a second, I was almost feeling like myself again, but I wasn't quite there yet realistically.

Fast-forwarding to the following week during the crossover service into 2018 on 31 December 2017, I was even more excited. Finally, the new year was approaching. I wanted to forget all about 2017 and just start afresh. Little did I know that 2018 was going to be more intense than anything I thought I went through in 2017.

Chapter 2

HELLO, 2018

Still excited about a new year, I wasn't due to be back in Coventry until 12 January 2018. As the days went by, the anxious thoughts started to come in. I had associated Coventry with negativity and bad energy, so I never wanted to be there. I had had a panic attack in the lift, and I had a small panic attack on the stairs, so how was I supposed to move around? Furthermore, throughout my stay in London for the Christmas break, the only place I went to was church on Sundays. Other than that, I barely went outside for even five minutes. However, let me tell you now there is nothing wrong with small and quiet Coventry. I was always homesick when there and was in such a rush to be back in London, but the anxiety-related challenges I experienced in Coventry were nothing compared to what I experienced when I moved back home to London in 2018. Shocking, right?

Although easier said than done, rather than entertaining worry and fear, this was a good opportunity for me to use one of my major coping strategies, which is the word of God, such as "Fear not, for I am with you; Be not be

Lois T.A. Omorayewa

dismayed, for I am your God. I will strengthen you, Yes, I will help you, I will uphold you with my righteous right hand" (Isa. 41:10 NKJV) and "Be of good courage, and He shall strengthen your heart, all you who hope in the Lord" (Ps. 31:24 NKJV). Thank God for growth, for now I know better. I fed off the likes of Isaiah 41:10 and others. I would read them to myself in third person, adding my name where appropriate. Now my studying and understanding the Bible has significantly increased and improved.

Back to the remaining two weeks I had left before going back to Coventry, during the first week of January 2018, my mum was to fly out of the country. It was a Sunday morning flight, and my dad and I were taking her to the airport before heading to church. I had anxious thoughts, especially the night leading up to Sunday morning, when I was getting ready. I was going to miss my mama so much, but that was not the reason for the anxious thoughts. I randomly remembered that when we got to Heathrow Airport to get to departures from the car park, we would have to go in the lift.

At this point, I still had not been in a lift since the first panic attack in November 2017 However, when we got to the airport, I was fine in the lift both when we were going into the airport and when leaving. I had wasted my time and energy worrying for no reason. That didn't take away the fear of going back to Coventry, although being able to get into that lift at Heathrow and being fine in it was relieving and I was glad I went because if I could avoid going, I would have. For the remaining days at home, I prayed a lot, begging God to help me and take me safely. I reminded him of how indecisive I was about whether or not

The Journey to Coventry

to pursue the master's degree. I also reminded him about how expensive it was to attend Warwick University and live in my accommodation—and how it was only by his grace that I was doing so.

There were quite a few justifiable reasons to not have gone for my master's, as intended, so I was certain that I was in alignment with God's will for me to be there at that point in time. At this point, my workload had already piled up and I should have started working on my dissertation, but I wasn't. However, I kept telling myself that I didn't know how but I was going to finish my master's and finish well. I don't know about other people, but from my experience, I realised I truly needed to guard my heart and my mind because anxiety had a way of making me have a very active mind, and this was not in a positive way. It felt as if I was always anticipating what the next unpleasant experience I would encounter would be. It also felt like being worried and scared of anxiety itself. It takes a lot of hard work, and there may be a bit of slipping here and there, but trust me when I say it is possible. It is OK to fall sometimes. If it were that easy, mental health would not be such a big issue, but when we fall, it is for us to rise, not stay down.

I love my parents so much, but during that period, I valued them even more for the type of upbringing I had. As I was growing up, they were strict, and I was literally raised in the way of the Lord. Now in my early twenties, I am confident that I won't go astray, especially not now, when I am making a consistent effort to ensure that God is the centre of my life going forward, no matter what. "Train up a child in the way he should go, and when he is old, he will not depart from it" (Prov. 22:6 NKJV).

For some people, this may be a popular scripture, but I want you to stop for a moment and truly take this scripture in and think about what it means. To my young readers, your parents may pray for you, but you have to take responsibility for your life. You have to open your mouth and speak to God about you! You have to speak life and good things into your life, destiny, and future. You should learn to develop the habit of looking in the mirror and affirming yourself, irrespective of what situation you find yourself in, because life will not always let you have it your way, whether you like it or not. I was in Coventry for several months, with no daddy and no mummy. It was just God and me; I couldn't see him, but I felt his presence on several occasions.

Eventually, I was able to get back to Coventry safely. The first couple of days back, I sometimes still experienced a racing heart going into the lift, but I used it anyway, and with time, I no longer was afraid of lifts. As the days went on, I wasn't great because there was still anxiety, even though I wasn't sure what exactly I was anxious about. However, I was OK. My eating had improved and so did my strength and energy levels. I was able to attend lectures and go to church again.

On 2 February 2018, my friends and I had planned to work on our coursework and/or dissertations during the day. Then, in the evening, we would go to the cinema. I was excited and decided I was going to dress up a bit, even though the cinema to our accommodation was just a five-minute drive. However, for me, that was the first time I was going out for fun since being in Coventry; prior to that, when I was out, it was either to university, groceries or

The Journey to Coventry

essentials shopping, GP appointments, or the gym initially before I fell ill, and the gym was less than a two-minute walk from my accommodation. I can't remember what time we planned to go to the cinema, but I remember sitting at my desk nearly all day. Then, during the last hour of working, I decided to snack on something before getting ready, as I had planned that I would have dinner when we were back from the cinema. I was having a malt drink and rich tea biscuit and suddenly started to have a weird stomach ache. It was surprising because apart from when I had the stomach tightness in October 2017 due to the stomach bug, I couldn't remember having any stomach discomfort.

However, this stomach pain quickly got so intense that I had to turn off the light and just turn on the bedside lamp and get in bed. While in bed, I was still feeling uncomfortable and continuously turning from side to side. I wanted to call my mum, but I didn't want her to get worried, so I decided to call my grandma, as during that period, she had prayed for me over the phone every day in the mornings before I went to lectures and at night before going to bed. The pain subsided as she prayed, and I was calmed. Eventually, the pain completely subsided. I stayed in bed for another hour, as I was still in a bit of shock as to what had happened. I kept contemplating whether to go to the cinema. My friend convinced me to come since the pain had gone, so I got dressed and went. In the cinema, I didn't buy any snacks, as I would usually do, because of the stomach incident. Even when we got back, although I was hungry, all I had was two slices of toast and butter—again, due to the fear of the stomach incident.

Fast-forwarding to Tuesday, 6 February 2018, one of my friends was in my room and we were working on our coursework. In the afternoon, we were both hungry and she said she felt like eating Jollof rice from a nearby African restaurant. I had eaten from there when I first got to Coventry and quite liked their food, so I decided I would have that too. We placed a phone order, went to pick it up, and returned to my room to eat. Within an hour or two of eating, I felt a weird pain in my stomach. It wasn't so painful, but I could feel the difference compared to how I felt before the pain. I thought, *Not today*. I initially didn't mention anything about the pain to my friend. I decided to cease working and lie in bed for a while.

The pain got intense, just like the last time and slightly even worse. My friend was still at the desk doing her coursework, and she was talking to me, but I was unable to respond properly, as I was in so much pain. She turned from the desk and saw how uncomfortable I looked. She started asking me questions. One thing I liked about the GP surgery I was registered with in Coventry was that you could call and request a call-back from doctor on the same day, which is not something that all GPs do. They might not call you back immediately, depending on their schedule and how busy they were, but they would definitely call you. I called the GP and requested a call-back. The call-back came just after 6 p.m., as I requested it quite late in the afternoon, which was when the incident took place. I explained to the doctor who called what had happened, and I was asked if I could quickly come into the practice, as they were going to close at 6.30 p.m. By this time, the pain had subsided, but I could still feel something in my stomach. I dreaded going to the GP, as I didn't think I was going anywhere else that day and

The Journey to Coventry

now I had to rush. However, I accepted the appointment, quickly ordered an Uber, and my friend and I left for the GP.

When I finally got to see the doctor, many questions were asked and some minor checks were carried out. The doctor then told me he suspected I had gallstones and he would refer me for a scan. My heart sank! What was that? I managed to keep myself composed and asked a few questions. Eventually, I was prescribed Buscopan to help with the stomach pain.

Back in my room now, I was alone; I decided to call my mum to tell her what had happened. As she answered the call, I wanted to start explaining what had happened. I don't know when I just burst out crying like a baby so that she could barely hear me initially. I was tired, so tired of it all. Life had not been the same since October 2017. We were now in February 2018; it was a new year. For how long was all this going to last? The transition from being so healthy to all these health challenges coming one after the other was too rapid. Eventually, I was able to put myself together and speak to my mum properly. She encouraged and prayed for me.

Later that night, I started doing a lot of googling on gallstones and saw something about the stomach pain that comes with gallstones occurring around the same time. Then it struck me: both times I experienced the stomach pains were around the same time, both around some minutes past 5 p.m. I wondered if I actually did have gallstones. I was so sad that night.

The next couple of days were tough; I was scared and hoping I didn't have gallstones. I was scared to eat properly, thinking I would have more stomach pain. However, as I mentioned earlier, when we fall, we are to rise. I had fallen, but I picked myself up. Don't get me wrong. The worries, thoughts, and fears did not just leave overnight, but I prayed and cried my heart out to God continuously. I also affirmed myself and made daily confessions. I reminded myself that "I [Lois] am more than a conqueror in all things through him who loves me" (Romans 8:37). *"If God is for me, who can be against me?"* (Romans 8:31 NKJV). I was also reminded in Romans 8:35 that "nothing can separate me from the love of Christ; not tribulation nor distress nor persecution, nothing" (NKJV). Therefore, no matter what I was going through, Jesus died for me, he loves me, and he is with me all the way—and what I don't understand, he fully understands and is in control.

I eventually had the scan, and as God would have it, the results came out clear. I did not have gallstones, and the second episode of the stomach pain that led to the scan was the last of such I experienced ever since. It was so relieving, and I gradually started to ease back into myself again instead of living in fear of the stomach pain reoccurring. The rest of February 2018 was rather good, with minimal challenges.

Then came March 2018. I completed quite a few modules in February 2018 and then in March 2018. I had no lectures scheduled, so this was a great opportunity to work on my coursework and dissertation. A few days into March 2018, I had a cold and sore throat and was not feeling great. Then one day during that period, I asked one of my friends

The Journey to Coventry

to come with me to get some medication from a nearby pharmacy. It was later during the day that I realised I was walking too fast so I could quickly get the medication and go back to my accommodation, as my friend had asked why I was walking so fast on our way to the pharmacy. Throughout these challenging periods, I experienced several bouts of agoraphobia whereby I only went out when I had to, such as going to lectures. Other than that, I was mostly indoors.

After a day or two from getting the medication for the cold and sore throat, another friend of mine and I had planned to go to a nearby mall, which was a five-minute walk or less from our accommodation. At the time, I still wasn't feeling great from the cold. I dreaded going, and when we were in the lift making our way downstairs, I said I didn't feel like going, but she insisted. Also, I was mostly the reason we were going, as I wanted to buy a pair of jeans, so I just agreed to go anyway.

When we got outside, we crossed the road to the other side, and we were then heading towards the mall when suddenly there was a weird sensation in my legs—nearly like a vibration from my legs upwards—and then a wave of nausea hit me. For a second, it felt like I either didn't know what was going on or I didn't know what I was doing, but it just didn't feel right. I suddenly stopped and told my friend something related to how I was feeling (which I have been trying to remember but can't). Suddenly, I just grabbed her hands and headed back to our accommodation. I went straight to lie on the bed. I felt calm again.

That started another cycle of not eating and not wanting to go out. Sometimes in a day, the "substantial" meal I would have for lunch or dinner would be two baby potatoes and stew. An anxious cycle had been formed since these challenges. First the triggers were mostly outside, and then I would feel uncomfortable and feel a wave of nausea. I would then rush back to my accommodation with a poor appetite and not wanting to go outside. It wasn't a pleasant experience. It was not a full-blown panic attack, but it was not any better if it was affecting the quality of my life on a daily basis.

I started considering coming back to London for a while, as I had no lectures for the entire March of 2018 until 9 April 2018. Furthermore, my main reason was that I knew that with what had happened on the way to the mall a few days into March, there was a high tendency that I would not even leave the second floor of my accommodation where I lived and definitely would not have been going outside, which I felt would only increase anxiety levels when I had lectures again in April. It was not as if I was going to be going out when back home in London, but at least I would move around the house from upstairs to downstairs, and vice versa, rather than staying in a room. Furthermore, even if I didn't go out, I would go to church every Sunday, which required a car journey compared to my church in Coventry, which was a minute walk. Finally, any opportunity for a change in my environment always sounded good because, as I mentioned earlier, I had subconsciously associated Coventry with negativity (I repeat, nothing is wrong with Coventry).

The Journey to Coventry

Eventually, I bought a train ticket to go to London. I had planned to meet my dad at work when he closed, and I could go home with him in the car. Also, I didn't have a key to my house yet, as we had just moved into a new house in January 2018. When it was time to board the train, as I got on the train and wheeled my suitcase to find my seat, I felt a churn in my stomach. Eventually, I found my seat; there was already someone next to me. I sat, held my Bible to my stomach, and was listening to prayer meditations all through the journey on an app called Abide. You don't have to be facing challenges to listen to it; it's very soothing if you are feeling stressed or just want to relax.

In case you are wondering what is it with me putting my Bible to my stomach, it is something that had become a habit since I was about nine or ten years old. One night while sleeping, I had a bad nightmare that made me run out of the room; I could not sleep again until my grandma told me to hold my Bible close to me in bed. I was then able to sleep again, and since then I always have my Bible close to me in bed. I hold my Bible to my stomach when flying or taking long road trips, and then I had not encountered anxiety. However, something about having a holy book containing God's promises and love to humanity made me feel safe since that night of the nightmare. It was therefore easy to adopt holding my Bible and feeling safe as a coping strategy when anxiety struck.

When the train got to London, I reached for my suitcase and alighted the train. London Euston train station was the station I used when going to or from Coventry. As I started walking towards exiting the platform, my stomach started to churn seriously; it was intense, and that was the first time I remember feeling very sick to my stomach. I paused for a few seconds and dialled a friend's number to distract myself. I continued walking, but at this point, there was no way I was taking the train to meet my dad at work. If you know London Euston train station, you will know how big and crowded it is, especially during rush hour, which was now fast approaching at that time. Furthermore, the train station is massive, and I still had a good couple of minutes of walking to do with several escalators to get through with a suitcase. The journey was also not going to be a straightforward one, as I would have to change trains and eventually board a bus, so I thought, *No, not today.*

I was now out of the platform and into the main train station. I then went to find out where I could get a taxi or Uber; at this point, the churning stomach had calmed down a little. I was directed to a place, and when I arrived there, I thought, *So I walked all this way to find only black taxis parked in some underground place.* I was certainly not going to take a black taxi, as they charge based on meter basis, which makes them quite expensive. Therefore, they were not ideal for long distances, which was my situation, and certainly not during rush hour in Central London. However, I kept walking towards them because I didn't know where I was going to go then. I was tired; due to the fear of the unknown, I had only had two slices of toast before leaving Coventry. The time had now gone past 4.30 p.m. I was supposed to meet my dad at 5.30 p.m., but now that I was not taking the train, there was most definitely going to be traffic. My head was all over the place. I just wanted to be in bed and breathe.

The Journey to Coventry

As I continued to approach the taxis, my stomach started to churn again. I felt so sick that I did not even realise my suitcase had burst open. Just as I got to one of the taxis, things started falling out of my suitcase. Oh, what a day! Ideally, I should have been frustrated, but I did not have the strength for that. I was just tired, so tired of it all. However, God sent help my way, which I remain thankful for. Two people were helping pick the stuff that fell out (they could see I wasn't feeling too well) while I stood there looking lost and telling them thank you. Eventually, I got help out of there and was able to call an Uber. Although there was traffic, I got to my dad around 6 p.m. I was OK and relaxed during the drive home. I got home safely all to the glory of God and to the shame of the devil. "Be strong and of good courage, do not fear nor be afraid of them; for the Lord your God, He is the one who goes with you. He will not leave you nor forsake you" (Deut. 31:6 NKJV). Indeed, he went with me, even though I was fearful and in discomfort at certain times. He did not leave me nor forsake me; he sent help my way and ensured I got home safely. Thank you, God.

Back home, I settled in well. This was the first time I was seeing the new house after moving, and I was happy and loved it. Then, a few days later, I was reflecting on the journey to London and everything that had happened, and I knew I would have to go back to Coventry in a couple of weeks' time, in April 2018. I then decided to call my GP in Coventry and request for a call-back from a doctor. Eventually, when the doctor called, it was fortunately the doctor that had suspected I had gallstones. It was easier to deal with him, as he had been in the loop of everything that had been going on. I narrated the incident that led to my deciding to come home and my experience coming back to London. He said that everything I said sounded like anxiety. I then asked if there was any medication I could use, and he said there were several medications but most of them would bring about the symptoms I was complaining about as side effects. After hearing that, I thought, *Never mind. I'm dealing with a lot already. The doctor said I should see if I am able to manage the symptoms or else I should call back.*

The rest of March was all right; I was mostly at home working on my coursework and dissertation. Soon it was leading up to the time to go back to Coventry. Due to my experience when coming to London, worry and fear creeped in. I started overanalysing on whether to go on Saturday or Sunday and what route to take. Eventually, I decided to go on Sunday after church, as it would make the journey shorter. I also requested that my mum follow me to the London Euston train station. After church on Sunday, I still had more than enough time, so we were just hanging around there.

Eventually, as the time was approaching, my dad drove us to the nearest train station, which was only about a five-minute drive away. As my mum and I got into the station, I was worried about two things. Firstly, I had not been on a train since coming home from Coventry a couple of weeks earlier. Secondly, I think I got too carried away that the estimated journey from the train station my dad dropped us at to London Euston was approximately thirty minutes. However, although it initially felt as if we had a lot of time to spare, we didn't leave church in enough time and there was a good chance I would miss my train.

The Journey to Coventry

When the train arrived, I got in and felt calm; it felt as though I was expecting something to have happened. I got to London Euston safely, but unfortunately, I had just missed my train. Initially, I felt upset and all over the place, but I calmed down and shortly after I was on another train to Coventry. I was totally fine on the train, so calm and relaxed that it was nearly too good to be true. I just listened to music and thanked God throughout the journey. Eventually, I was back in my room. I was excited that night, although I was already missing home. I was excited about the smooth journey, which gave me confidence about going into university the next day and having lectures that week, especially after not having lectures for an entire month.

April and May 2018 were my best times in Coventry because I was getting ready to leave for good. I couldn't wait. I would look at the calendar every other day, counting down. Although my course was for one year, my modules ended in May, so from that point onwards, I was meant to complete any coursework that was still left and then work on my dissertation until August 2018. My last lecture was on 18 May, and by noon on 19 May, I was out and headed back home to London. I had asked my dad a couple of days back if he could pick me up on 20 May. He wasn't going to be available that weekend but would be available the following week; however, I couldn't wait. I had all my things packed; I was going home that weekend by fire by force, and whenever my dad was ready, we would come and pick my things up together.

Deciding to complete my dissertation at home in London was not the easiest decision to make. Normally I was a library person and never liked working from home.

However, although that had changed in October 2018, my friends and I mostly sat together to get our university work done and motivated and made ourselves accountable for each other. Being in London meant that I would have to do it by myself at home. Also, it was mandatory that students were in regular contact with their supervisors. There was even a log on our university intranet where supervisors had to log each meeting they had with their supervisees. My supervisor preferred face-to-face meetings, which meant that even if I left Coventry, I would still have to come back often to see him. Furthermore, he was also worried about my going home to work on my dissertation. Due to potential distractions from family and friends, he said that he usually got worried when his students said they wanted to work on their dissertations from home. I explained to him why I wanted to work from home and assured him I was not going to be distracted, and he approved of my going home. I didn't know how things were going to be working from home, but I knew that staying in Coventry would only make me stay indoors, which would only increase my anxiety levels.

"Now faith is the substance of things hoped for, the evidence of things not seen" (Heb. 11:1). "My soul, wait silently for God alone, For my expectation is from him" (Ps. 62:5 NKJV).

I did my first degree in London and did not live at home but pretty much opposite the campus, as I was always doing all my studying in the university and my room was mostly for relaxing and sleeping, especially during exams. Whenever I was going home during my first degree, I knew I wasn't going to be as productive with my work,

The Journey to Coventry

and I usually didn't stay at home for too long except it was summer holidays. Therefore, with this demanding dissertation that was worth 50 per cent of my master's degree, I wasn't exactly sure how it was going to go at home, but I knew God had brought me that far for a reason, for when I first started experiencing health challenges, it was as though my mind was constantly in battle. One voice would be saying something along the lines of *It's still early. Why don't you forget this master's and go back to London or, better still, defer this master's? You can always come back in a year's time to finish.* And another voice would remind me how indecisive I was about doing this master's, but I had developed a strong interest in project management since halfway through the second year of my first degree. The other voice would say, *No! You are going to finish this master's and you will be OK.*

Therefore, I knew that as long as I continued to wait on God and do my part, which was being committed to finishing well and working hard towards finishing well, God would come through for me. I was also reminded that I had completed a coursework during March 2018 when I came home in London after the small panic attack on the way to the mall. I achieved a distinction in that module, so I was encouraged.

Chapter 3

THE RETURN HOME

I was so happy to be home. Things started improving; I gradually started eating well again, gaining weight and having so much energy, although initially I was still staying indoors except on Sundays, when we went to church. Also, working on my dissertation was initially hard. Although I was behind my initial dissertation schedule and milestones that I had planned, I gave myself about two days off. I needed it. I needed to rest. I needed to clear my head so I could be productive. It was still May, yet so much had already happened in 2018, and somehow with the help of God, I managed to complete ten modules and was now facing the final hurdle: my dissertation.

The break helped. Then I had a conversation with myself: *Girl, you have to do what you have to do, we are nearly there. Lois, you are going to finish well.* It was not exactly easy, especially during the hot summer, but I pushed hard. I would get out of bed in the morning between 6.30 and 7, get in the shower and get ready, and then sit at my desk and work on my dissertation through the day. Depending

The Journey to Coventry

on the day, how I felt, and how much I had gotten done, I wouldn't close for the day until ten or eleven at night, even a few times until midnight. However, I made sure to take regular breaks throughout the day. That was my routine every day except weekends. Saturdays I did chores in the morning but still worked on my dissertation alongside doing other things through the day. On Sundays after church, I would eat, take a nap, and start working on my dissertation. There were a few Sundays when, after taking a nap, I was still too tired to work on my dissertation, and I would think, *I can't kill myself. No point sitting at the desk and not getting anything done.* So, I ensured I rested on such Sundays because the next day was going to be an early start.

By June 2018, I thought that this dissertation was demanding in different forms, but I needed to start finding time to job hunt. I started completing jobs applications which were long and tiring and at the same time completing a 22,000-word dissertation which also entailed my interviewing close to thirty project managers and transcribing and analysing every single interview. Even though I was doing everything indoors, life was extremely busy.

Towards the end of June, I landed my first interview. I was both nervous and excited at the same time. One thing about applying for jobs during that stressful dissertation period was that I would have accepted the first offer I received. Attending interviews was expensive and time-consuming. If I remember clearly, during all the interviews I attended, it took me no less than one hour making the journey each way. Furthermore, although I wanted to be wealthy, at that point, I wanted experience more than

Lois T.A. Omorayewa

anything else, so as long as I got a graduate starting salary, that was fine. However, experience was first for now, as the only substantial experience on my CV at the time was the internship I did in the summer leading up to my final year as an undergraduate and right after graduating and they were both in the same place.

I attended the interview, and if I remember clearly, that was my first time going out on my own again in London since the health challenges started. Normally it would be either church with family or travelling to or from Coventry. The interview went well; I liked the place and people. I thought that this might just be it, only to get told that there was nothing I could have done better but they found someone who had experience in that field and he was available to start immediately, whereas I didn't have any relevant experience and was not available to start until September 2018, when my dissertation was completed and my master's degree was officially achieved.

There was also a second unsuccessful interview with another company and then a third unsuccessful interview with yet another company. The third interview got me emotional. A recruiter had contacted me, and it was a long process. I sent my CV off; I had an informal telephone interview; I had to create a sixty-second video saying why I thought I was suitable for the job; and I had to attend an assessment day that consisted of a group activity, a written role play, an oral play, and a one-on-one interview. Then, finally, there was a second interview. The interviews with the third company were my hardest; they really drilled me. They asked me questions about doing complex operational activities that I would ideally want to think about and

The Journey to Coventry

analyse before giving an answer. However, the interviewer expected answers within seconds.

The next morning, I was told I had not gotten the job because I had not elaborated on some of my answers as much as they would have liked. I was upset. I had spent so much time through this process, and I had to go the company twice; meanwhile, I still had a dissertation to complete. I cried. This particular rejection hurt so much, but what I did not know was that God was preparing me for the one.

"And we know that all things work together for the good of those who love God, to those who are called according to his purpose" (Rom. 8:28 NKJV).

"Trust in the Lord with all your heart, and lean not on your own understanding; in all your ways acknowledge Him, and he shall direct your paths" (Prov. 3:5–6 NKJV).

From the first day I got to Coventry for my master's, I consistently prayed to God that I would get a job before I finished my master's degree. However, when graduate schemes were opened for applications, I could not apply as a result of my health, and even if I could, how was I supposed to attend interviews in the initial state I was in? I wanted to work in London, which would have also meant quite a few Coventry to London journeys, and vice versa, for interviews. After a few of the challenges early in 2018, there were several times I wondered how I would be able to get a job with the whole anxiety situation, but I never stopped praying the prayer about getting a job before finishing my master's degree. At the time of the third job rejection, it was already early August 2018 and my dissertation was due on 20 August 2018. I had to defend it on 3 September 2018, which also officially marked the end of my master's degree, but still I never stopped praying that I would get a job before my master's ended. You will agree with me that getting a job is not always easy. To be honest, at that point in time, because it was already August and I had now paused job hunting to complete and polish up and print my dissertation, which I had to travel to Coventry to submit in person, getting a job before 3 September 2018 was not looking realistic. However, "Jesus said to him, If you believe, all things are possible to him who believes" (Mark 9:23 NKJV). Therefore, I thought it wasn't God's will for me to have a job just yet, and although I wasn't guaranteed, it was not impossible. Therefore, as unrealistic as it looked, it was possible.

During the application period with the company I had my third interview with, I was on LinkedIn one day and came across a job posting with a huge organisation. I completed an online application process without thinking much of it. A couple of days later, I received an email requesting a telephone interview and one was scheduled. A few days prior to the interview, I opened up the company's website to prepare for the interview, but the company is large, with a parent company and several sub-brands and so on. I was confused going through the website and closed the link. The last two to three weeks of my dissertation was not the period to waste time. The telephone interview was for a Monday morning, so the Sunday before that Monday, after my usual postchurch rest, I spent the evening preparing for the phone interview, which I felt went well.

The Journey to Coventry

On the day I got rejected from the company with which I had my second interview, the rejection came in just before 9.30 a.m. I wasn't in a great mood that day at all, but I managed to pull myself together and say a little word of prayer about the rejection. On the same day, at 4.26 p.m., the company I came across for their job posting on LinkedIn contacted me, to invite me for a face-to-face interview as a result of a successful telephone interview. Initially, there was no excitement. However, by the next day, I started to get over the second rejection and started to see this interview invite as another opportunity. This was the only interview I had left at that point, and out of all the previous companies I had interviewed with, this company aligned to the type of career I wanted the most. They had better opportunities for growth (at least based on what I had read and seen about all the three companies), and the pay was way above my expectations of a graduate starting salary, which was a huge bonus. None of these were going to pass me by. "Behold, I am the Lord, the God of all flesh. Is there anything too hard for me?" (Jer. 32:27 NKJV). No, Father, nothing at all. I intensified my prayers. I liked what I was learning about the company so far, and I was already tired of sending in applications that sometimes weren't even responded to.

I prepared a lot for the interview, and on the day of the interview, I fell in love with the company. It was beautiful. The two interviewers made me feel comfortable and were nice to me. The interview lasted nearly two hours. They acknowledged that the company was quite complex (as I had thought from going through their website) and spent the first hour just telling me all about the company. There was so much information to take in, but already I wanted this job. "Wisdom is the principal thing; Therefore, get wisdom. And in all your getting, get understanding" (Prov. 4:7 NKJV). This time around, for every question asked during the interview, I elaborated on my answers well. I made sure I was understood and even gave examples with my answers. After the interview, I went back home feeling good about it but did not want to get too excited so as not to be disappointed again.

From that day going forward, I intensified my prayers even more; I really wanted the job. "But if we hope for what we do not see, we eagerly wait for it with perseverance" (Rom. 8:25 NKJV). One thing about the application process with this company that was different to the previous two companies that I had interviewed with that they took their time in responding to me. Therefore, there was a lot of suspense during the entire process; I just made sure it did not affect the final stage of my dissertation.

I got a response from the company six days after the interview, but it was not a certain response. The recruiter who had carried out the telephone interview with me earlier, before the face-to-face interview, emailed me, asking how I found the interview. She also said the interviewers really liked me but were still carrying out some more interviews before they could give feedback to me on the next steps. This was on 20 August 2018, the day my dissertation was due for online submission. "Pray without ceasing. In everything give thanks; for this is the will of God in Christ Jesus for you" (1 Thess. 5:17–18 NKJV). I thanked God for the response; although I did not want to get too excited, at least it was not a straight rejection. I continued to pray.

Chapter 4

HERE COMES THE SETTLEMENT

Finally, I submitted my dissertation online on 20 August 2018, but I needed to print two hard copies and submit in person, and it needed to be the same as what I submitted online, from the beginning to the end. I bought a train ticket to go to Coventry for the 22 August 2018. Early on the previous day, I made my way to Queen Mary University of London, where I completed my first degree to have my dissertation printed ahead of my next day's journey to Coventry. When I got to the Copy Shop, as it is called, I placed my order and was told to come back after two hours. I had planned to go to a nearby mall which was only a five-minute train ride away because I knew I would have to wait for some time for my hard copies to be ready and it didn't make sense going all the way back home and coming back again.

I made my way to the mall. I was going to treat myself that day; I had worked so hard through all these challenges with the help of God. When I got to the mall, I felt overwhelmed and a bit emotional. When I was in Queen Mary, I visited that mall regularly, but there I was walking around the mall for the first time in a year with no fear of a panic attack, when just a few months earlier, I didn't even step outside except when I needed to. However, I was now shopping for myself while 50 per cent worth of my master's degree was being printed for submission; I felt so free. Everything was becoming fine again. Everything went well. My dissertation was now fully completed and submitted. All that was left was for me to defend my dissertation.

Back to the job application process ... Ten days after the initial response from the company, I was invited for a second interview to which I confirmed I was going to attend. The next day, I sent an email to the recruiter asking for more information about my second interview, as I was also required to make a presentation at the interview. Upon sending the email, I immediately got an automatic response stating that she no longer worked with the company. *What a time*, I thought. To cut a long story short, after a series of phone calls and emails, I was finally passed on to another recruiter. However, it was just a few days to my dissertation defence, and this was as important as the degree because I needed to pass my defence to pass my dissertation, irrespective of the dissertation grade, and I needed to pass my dissertation to be awarded a master's degree. Therefore, I put preparations for the interview aside initially.

Thankfully, my dissertation defence on 3 September 2018 went well, and although I was not told my exact grade, as it was just provisional until confirmed by the exam board, I was told my grade boundary was a merit. I was happy it was finally over.

The Journey to Coventry

The same day, on 3 September 2018, after returning to London from my defence in Coventry, I ate, had a good rest, and then started preparing for my second interview. Preparing for the second interview entailed preparing a presentation on how I would implement a global project (which was a real project the company had carried out). It was mostly about this interview until the actual day came, which was 6 September 2018.

A day before the interview, I had a phone call with the new recruiter I was now dealing with. He told me that I shouldn't worry about it, that they were happy with my project management aspect of things but they wanted to know whether I was a good fit for the team, as people were very important to them. He further said that I would get the opportunity to meet some team members and interact well with them. He also said that there shouldn't be interview-style questions in this interview and it should just be the PowerPoint presentation and meeting some other members of the team. I prepared for everything—the PowerPoint presentation and the kinds of questions I would want to ask the other members of the team—and I did some preparations for interview-style questions.

On my arrival at the company for my second interview, I was nicely received from reception by one of the interviewers to where the interview was going to take place. It was a small room, and as soon as I walked into the room, I saw a man sitting down. He was a senior staff, CIO (chief information officer). In my head, I was, like, *Sorry, what? Why did no one tell me about this?*

Anyway, I felt welcome and comfortable. The next thing I knew, the CIO started asking me interview-style questions. I was initially shocked, but by the end of the interview, even I knew I did well. There were a few times I was nearly running out of breath because of how much I was elaborating on my answers. After that, the CIO left and my two interviewers then took me to another room, where I gave my presentation. They then asked me a few informal questions relating to role and company. Then, towards the end, one of the interviewers asked me if I would take job if it was offered. I said yes and explained why I would. The interview ended, and they said they would get back to me in a couple of days. I continued to pray while awaiting their response. I was available to start working the following Monday, even though I really needed some time off; it had been a long year, with still a few months to go.

On 12 September 2018, I was quite busy. Three of my friends from Coventry were coming to visit me, and I was cooking for them. When I finished cooking and was awaiting their arrival, I checked my email and received an email from the job recruiter, apologising for the delay in getting back to me and saying they were rounding up the recruitment process and I was still coming close to the top of the ratings. Wow, I was a little excited but nervous. I prayed to get the job. They were recruiting for two people, so I prayed to be one of them.

"But may the God of all grace, who called us to his eternal glory by Christ Jesus, after you have suffered a while, perfect, establish, strengthen and settle you" (1 Pet. 5:10 NKJV).

The Journey to Coventry

My friends came, and I pushed the excitement and tension of that email aside. It was so good to see them and catch up again and, importantly, we were now free—no more university deadlines and stressing over coursework or dissertations. Towards the evening, my phone rang. I answered it but could not really hear the caller, so I excused myself from the living room and went into the kitchen. It was the recruiter calling. I did not know how to feel. We exchanged pleasantries, and then he asked what type of salary I was looking for. I explained that I was not salary driven but more experience driven and so on. He then asked if I would like to work for the company and where they were on my list. I told him they were my top preference and I would like to work there, explaining why. The next thing I heard was that the company would like to offer me the job ... and congratulations. I wanted to scream, but I had to compose myself. I had to ask him what he had just said, and he repeated himself and said more things. At that point, I wasn't composed enough to take in everything he was saying.

For the next couple of days, I was overwhelmed, but the first night, I couldn't sleep even when I tried. I kept thanking God and smiling. My life felt in order; based on my dissertation and modules grades, I had achieved a master's degree in programme and project management with a merit; moreover, I had just secured a good job at a reputable company. All of this, despite how tough the year had been ... On the Sunday of that week, I gave a testimony in church about all of these happenings.

Chapter 5

NOT SO FAST! —THE TRAINING SCHOOL

My start date at work was 1 October 2018. This meant I had about two weeks to relax and get ready for work. My life had not felt this in order since the whole challenge started. It was just my dad and me in the house towards the end of September 2018. My mum was out of the country, and my brother had gone back to uni. My dad was also due to travel out in the next couple of days, meaning I was going to be home alone for nearly two weeks. This was going to be the first time I'd ever slept in an entire house alone, but eventually I had to learn. However, I was also going away for one of the weekends. I had coincidentally booked a weekend away to Paris in October with two of my friends.

Three days before my dad was due to travel, I wanted to go to a shopping centre that was about a five-minute bus ride or fifteen-minute walk. However, we were expecting a delivery that day, so I had to be home until I received the delivery. The delivery came earlier than expected. I was a little hungry and wanted to get McDonald's, which

The Journey to Coventry

was less than a two-minute walk away from the house. I then said to myself that it was better for me to go to the shopping centre first and hit McDonald's on my way back so I could enjoy it, relax, and not have to worry about going out again, especially because sometimes when I eat and am full and satisfied, I tend to feel sleepy and lazy, especially with McDonald's food.

I went to the shopping centre; I was done quickly and ready to go home. There were three major buses that served the shopping centre. Two of the buses were single-deckers, while one of the buses was a double-decker. Usually it was the bus 174, which was a double-decker that took me to and from the shopping centre. As I was walking towards the bus stop, I saw a double-decker bus and ran for it, boarding it and thinking it was my usual 174 bus. However, this time around, it was one of the single-decker buses that was replaced with a double-deck bus, for whatever reason. As soon as I realised I was on the wrong bus, I pressed the buzzer so I could get off at the next bus stop. I got off at the next bus stop and started to walk towards the closest 174 bus stop there. The 174, when taking me back home, should have taken a left turn, whereas the other bus took a right turn.

Just a few steps after getting off the wrong bus, I suddenly felt a weird sensation in my leg, followed by a wave of nausea. I heard myself exclaim out loud. I was so confused. It was like the same experience I'd had in Coventry on the way to the mall earlier on in March 2018. What had just happened? What was going on? I had been going out, especially to this shopping centre, so what was the problem? I had no stressor at that point in time, and I wasn't anxious about anything—at least not that I knew of. My appetite was fantastic, and I had gained so much weight again and looked healthier. There were so many thoughts and questions flooding my mind as I waited at the bus stop uncomfortably. Eventually, the bus came, and I boarded it, got off at my stop, walked home, and quickly got in bed. This was yet again the same cycle, except that this did not make any sense. What had just happened? I was trying to convince myself that it was all in my head. I even called my brother and asked whether running for a bus should make you feel off; he was confused, and at the time, I had not told him what had happened, as I was still trying to comprehend it myself. My appetite was knocked out. From planning to have McDonald's, I think I had only two slices of toast the entire day. I was shocked and worried; this was one week after the testimony I shared in church and a week before I was due to start my new job.

Interestingly, a day before this incident, I went to get something in a big Tesco not too far away from my house. After that, I walked to a nearby Argos to purchase and pick up a mirror I had reserved. Initially, I had thought I would use an Uber to get back home because of the mirror. However, when I was given the mirror, it was not as heavy as I had anticipated, so I felt I could manage on the bus. I went to a bus stop that was less than a five-minute walk and then realised the bus was in eleven minutes; I wasn't prepared to wait for that. I thought, *Can't I just walk?* It was about a fifteen-minute walk, and worst-case scenario, if I got so tired because of the mirror, I would stop at the next bus stop and take the bus. I started walking, and I was fine. As I approached a shortcut towards home after already walking for some minutes, I remember talking aloud to

The Journey to Coventry

myself, saying something along the lines of "Wow, so this is really me walking this distance with a box containing a standing mirror. So I am finally healed. Thank you, Jesus." I arrived home safely, not even tired, and set my mirror up. "Oh, that men would give thanks to the Lord for his goodness, and his wonderful works to the children of men" (Ps. 107:8 NKJV). Having experienced this just a day before, to now experiencing what I experienced after getting off the wrong bus, I didn't understand what was going on.

Well, I had prayed for this job, so nothing was stopping me. On 1 October 2018, I was up early and got dressed for work. It was my first day, so I had booked a taxi to take me to the nearest train station, which was under a ten-minute drive. I then boarded the train towards the direction I was going to, and for some odd reason, I thought to myself that I was fine (referring to being OK on the train). It was as if I had just jinxed things by having that thought; it couldn't have been more than five minutes after that suddenly my stomach started to feel funny. It was not pain or cramps; the only way I could instinctively describe it was a nervous stomach with uncomfortable butterflies. Yes, I was a little nervous; it was my first day at my first proper job. However, I knew myself. No matter how nervous I was, aside from a racing heart, there was usually no other symptom. Interestingly, my heart was not even racing at the time, and I never had any stomach issues until the start of my challenges in October 2018. Therefore, I was almost 100 per cent sure that this had nothing to do with the nervousness and was more like anxiety. I was right. When I eventually got to the closest train station near my new workplace, I came out and was walking towards the location. It was a short walk, and because I had been there twice for the two interviews,

Lois T.A. Omorayewa

I knew where I was going, but suddenly my stomach was churning even more.

My first day at work was great, except for what I was battling internally. My stomach felt uncomfortable the entire day. Throughout the day, I would tighten my stomach and then release it to see if it felt better, but that didn't make much difference. It was my first day. I felt the need to just learn to deal with it. During lunchtime, some of my team members invited me to come with them to a shop to get some food and to show me around. Work is around London Bridge, which is such a beautiful area. I wasn't going to buy anything, but I decided to go with them to get outside again because of what had happened earlier on, on my way to work. As we walked and chatted, I was fine. I was a little nervous but wasn't panicking; the only thing was that it was quite cold, so I was shivering a little. That walk during the lunch gave me a bit more confidence to go home. I got home safely, but my appetite had been affected yet again. I had toast and ginger-and-lemon tea before leaving for work in the morning, only ate a banana at work, and now I was only going to have two small potatoes and stew for dinner. The next day, Tuesday, that five-minute walk to work from London Bridge station made my stomach churn yet again, but thankfully it was a better day—no uncomfortable stomach the entire day. Once I got to work, the symptoms eased off nearly immediately.

Either Wednesday or Thursday, when I got out of the train station as usual and was taking that walk to work, I expected to feel something in my stomach, but I felt nothing and was shocked. I remember being overwhelmed and just looking straight-ahead and saying *Thank you, Jesus* silently, also

The Journey to Coventry

asking that the churning stomach not start again. "The name of the Lord is a strong tower; the righteous run to it and are safe" (Prov. 18:10 NKJV).

I started to worry about one thing: my first work weekend was coincidentally the weekend I had planned to go to Paris with my friends. How was I going to travel like this? How was I going to move around without triggering a churning stomach? How would I eat? All these questions and more filled my mind, but I was not going to opt out of the journey; bookings had been made and paid for. My girls really wanted to go on holiday, and we had chosen this date to suit me, based on when my master's would be complete, so I wasn't going to disappoint them. God would make a way; I would be OK. "And he said, 'My Presence will go with you, and I will give you rest'" (Exod. 33:14 NKJV).

Eventually, I made it to Paris safely and had a lovely time with my friends. I was able to move around without panic attacks, and thankfully, my eating improved, so I was no longer eating just two small potatoes when I got back to London.

There were two routes I could use to work. The one I had been using during my first week at work was the one that had the five-minute walk from the train station to work, and vice versa. For the second route, I would get off at a different train station and would get on a bus to work which was approximately a ten-minute bus ride if there was no traffic. The good thing about using this second bus route in the mornings was that the bus stop where I was supposed to get off at was only a two-minute walk to work, unlike the five-minute walk from the train station of the first route to work. However, with the second route, when leaving work, I had to walk for five minutes, as the opposite bus stop taking me back to the train station that would take me home was located in front of the train station from the first route. However, it was still OK because this was taking me to London Liverpool Street station, which was the first train station the train towards my house took off from so, I was guaranteed a seat.

I started taking the second route, as explained above. Days after, I started noticing that I was fine when going to work in the morning, but when leaving work at the end of the day, I was anxious taking that five-minute walk to the bus stop, and once I had gotten to the bus stop, I would feel a bit relieved. It wasn't comfortable, but it wasn't bad either, as that didn't stop me from still walking down that route at the end of every weekday that I was at work.

It got to the point that depending on who was available, I would call either my best friend or my brother just before I exited the building so that I would be distracted. At the time, only the two of them knew about this new route-related anxiety. I felt this occurrence was strange, but it wasn't so bad; at least it didn't affect my appetite or bring about any other symptoms. The only thing was that I was always anxious during the walk, but once I had gotten through it, I would be fine again. I kept telling myself that the more I walked down that route, the better things would get and I would no longer feel anxious when walking that route. "Have I not commanded you? Be strong and of courage; do not be afraid, nor be dismayed, for the Lord your God is with you wherever you go" (1 Josh. 1:9 NKJV).

The Journey to Coventry

However, I started thinking about doing something about the situation. I started googling things. I then started considering counselling, specifically for cognitive behaviour therapy (CBT), which is usually highly recommended for anxiety. I had referred myself for talking therapies, which is provided by the NHS (National Health Service), but I had been told about how long the waiting list could be. I then started looking for short-term counselling privately until the NHS would have a slot for me (as I write this, I am still on the waiting list). Face-to-face counselling privately was very expensive, so I then started looking for online ones, but they were also expensive. I then came across one that rather struck me, called Faithful Counselling. The cost, although not cheap, was reasonable in comparison to other online counselling services I had found. I signed up but didn't subscribe to any counselling plan, yet I was matched with a counsellor within an hour.

Chapter 6
ANXIETY SEASON 2

On the morning of 24 October 2018, while having my usual lemon-and-ginger tea and toast before heading to work, I didn't know if I took too big of a gulp of the tea at some point, but there was a weird sensation and it nearly went the wrong way. I made my way to work fine. When it was time to go home, the anxiety started kicking in earlier than usual; I had texted my brother to see if he was available for a quick call. He immediately called me, asking if I was OK, as he knew about the anxiety when going home. I told him I would call him once I left the building. As I left the building, I called him on FaceTime, and as we were talking, suddenly the connection went off, but I carried on walking.

For some strange reason, as I got close to the bus stop, I started to feel anxious, and the closer I got, the farther away it seemed. There was a rush of adrenaline, and a few seconds to the bus stop, I felt a sensation I still can't explain. I could feel a wave of nausea coming. I increased my pace and got to the bus stop and quickly sat down. I started considering if I should take an Uber home, but

The Journey to Coventry

London Bridge station is a very busy area; I didn't know the pickup locations at the time, and that was not the time to start walking the street looking for an Uber driver. Previously, on one occasion, the bus that usually took me from the London Bridge station to London Liverpool Street station was on diversion and was coming in twenty-three minutes. I usually checked the bus time before leaving work. After seeing that it would be twenty-three minutes, I thought, *No way*. I then decided to order an Uber to take me to Liverpool Street. Eventually, we spent about fifteen minutes looking for each other, to no avail, and he cancelled the trip, so I ended up walking to the bus stop and taking the bus. Remembering this occurrence during whatever it was that was going on put me off ordering an Uber, so I decided to proceed with public transport home.

When I got on the bus, still feeling on edge, I called my grandmother to pray for me. She was worried and asking questions, but I just gave her a hint of what was going on and asked her to pray that I get home safely, saying I would explain later. I was sitting next to someone on the bus, there were people around me, the bus was quite packed, and I didn't want to draw attention to myself. When I was asking my grandmother to pray for me, I was saying it in Yoruba. She prayed, and the call ended. All through, I kept on praying silently, *God please help me get home safely*. When I got to the train station, I got off the bus and then walked for less than a minute. When I went down the escalator towards where I usually boarded my train, I started to feel funny again. I quickly found somewhere close by to sit while trying to squint to see what time the next train was due and what platform, as a few platforms were dedicated to this particular train that took me home, and vice versa.

Eventually, I was able to get on the train. I was very uncomfortable, yet I was trying to keep still because I did not want to attract any attention. The journey felt so slower and longer than usual. I texted my brother, narrating what had happened. He called me shortly after, and I asked him if he could stay on the phone until I got home, to which he agreed. Although he was on the phone, I was barely talking; I was uncomfortable, and he just kept on asking if I was OK. When I got to the stop where I was going to get off, I could feel the sensations coming back and I was feeling on edge more intensely. I told my brother that I was about to get off the train and he should tell me everything was going to be OK, and he did continuously. Although I was not feeling good, I was able to make it out of the train station safely and straight into a taxi office to get a taxi home. I was told that I would have to wait for fifteen minutes, so I sat there waiting while on the phone to my brother. At this point, I was able to speak a bit more than when I was on the train. Eventually, I made it home safely. Normally when I got back from work, I'd take a shower, but that day I just laid in bed. I was hurt and confused. For how long was this going to go on? What had I done wrong to deserve this? I had not even spent a month at work.

At that point in time, it was hard to pray, but I knew God could hear my silent cry. I desperately wanted to be well and OK. I wanted to leave a normal life and do things I wanted rather than living in fear. For me, proper adulthood was just starting, as I was no longer in university and was now a working-class woman.

The Journey to Coventry

At this point, I knew I had to let my parents know what was going on. I also knew that going to work the following day, especially using the same route and so on, was not a good idea, so I needed to ask my manager if it was OK to work from home on Thursday and Friday and return to work the following Monday. I thought this would give me time to let things calm down. It was hard texting my manager to ask for time off; it had been under a month since I started working. It was too early, in my opinion, to start taking time off—but health first. I had to do what I had to do.

I sent my line manager a text message explaining the situation to him and asked if I could work from home the next day and the day after and resume back at the office the following Monday; he agreed. I had also started to think I really needed to speak to a professional about all those panic attacks. I can't remember the time interval, but I got an email from Faithful Counselling that I had signed up for two days earlier, but I had not subscribed to any of the counselling plans. Faithful Counselling were offering me a seven-day free trial—oh, what perfect timing. "God is our refuge and strength, a very present help in trouble" (Ps. 46:1 NKJV).

I sent a message to my assigned counsellor, giving a brief explanation of things, and asked when was the earliest we could schedule a session which could be in the form of a phone call or a video call. She responded, and a session was scheduled for Friday.

Later that day, I found out that my mum had just been promoted at work. The promotion was long overdue, and it was very stressful. It involved both a written and oral examination. I had been praying for this promotion way before they had a clue of when the exam invitation would be out. On the day of the exam, I fasted; my mum regularly fasts whenever I have something important going on. There was so much negative news flying about while they were awaiting the results, and I remember always encouraging my mum and telling her to stop listening to negative rumours. I would then go back to God and speak to him on my mum's behalf. To think God finally answered our prayers and that one of the happiest days for my mum was one of the saddest days for me ... I was happy to hear the news, but I was quite numb to express it. I wondered if I was supposed to tell my mum about the panic attack on this type of day that should be one of celebration for my family.

Eventually, my parents got to find out what was going on but didn't really understand it. I remember my dad asking me if I was sleeping well, eating well, and so on. I remember responding to him, saying yes and that I was fine. I further said that I didn't understand what was going on, but I knew I wasn't ill but would just work from home on Thursday and Friday, then go back to work the following Monday, as I had told my manager. Funnily enough, without knowing the Wednesday incident was going to happen, I had already taken permission from my manager to work from home on Friday to enable me to register with a GP. The one I wanted to register with was about a three-minute walk from my house. I had visited there about a week earlier on my way back from work one day to enquire about registering. However, I was told that new patients were only registered between 11 a.m. and 12 a.m.

The Journey to Coventry

The next day, Thursday, I woke up alright; I thought I was fine. When my dad was leaving for work, I was talking to him and even followed him outside until he left. I came back into the house and went upstairs to my room, but I started to feel funny; I felt tired and weak. *What is this again?* I thought. I then decided to call the GP I had initially enquired about registering with. I was told I could register that day but would be unable to get an appointment to see a doctor until two or three weeks and would also need to have a health check before I could see a doctor. I spent half of the day calling almost every GP in the area, as I really wanted to see a doctor that day. At the same time, I was trying to work. Thankfully, even when I was in the office, about 90 per cent of my meetings were online and mostly through Skype for business, as we are a global company and a typical meeting would involve people from different countries. I unfortunately did not have my work laptop; I wasn't expecting Wednesday's incident, so after work, I had put my laptop in my locker as I usually did before leaving the office.

I had already missed my standard 10 a.m. meeting every weekday, when we would review the progress of our projects. This particular meeting is not usually on Skype for business but a different app, and I had difficulties downloading the app on my personal laptop. I had used my laptop all through my first and second degree, and there was so much on it that it was working slowly. I was panicking about work so much; it was too early for all of this. I had not even spent one month there yet, and I was on probation for three months. One of the agreements I had signed in my contract was that during probation, either party could terminate the contract at any point in time.

"And which of you by worrying can add one cubit to his stature? If you then are not able to do the least, why are you anxious for the rest" (Luke 12:25–26 NKJV).

"Therefore, do not worry about tomorrow, for tomorrow will worry about its own things. Sufficient for the day is its own trouble" (Matt. 6:34 NKJV).

Have you ever heard the saying that health is wealth? It literally is; there is no better way of saying it. God knew we would experience challenges, which is why he was telling us that worrying was not going to be beneficial to any challenges life throws at us. "The Lord also will be a refuge for the oppressed, A refuge in times of trouble" (Ps. 9:9 NKJV). One thing about my experience that I would love for people to not go through is worrying. I worried a lot, I feared a lot, I had negative rumination about many things like panic attacks, and I am good with remembering dates, but it was not a positive thing in this situation. I worried a lot about my job, but what was worrying going to do, get me back in the office? At this point, I must also mention that you shouldn't put things like work before your health. When you need to look after yourself, please do it to the best of your ability. I wasn't feeling my best but was always worrying and stressing about work as if it could help the situation. Eventually, it got to the stage where I had to start telling myself that only the living can work—and it's true. Of course, worry does not go away overnight. And we are humans, so from time to time, we might feel the need to worry, but worrying is exhausting and a mood reducer. Worrying makes you only see what is wrong and what could potentially go wrong. As I write this, I am also speaking to myself because I know I still have a lot to work on in this area.

The Journey to Coventry

Back to finding a GP, I eventually found one that was willing to get me registered that day and have me seen by a doctor that same day as an emergency, without first having a health check done, although I was told I would have to have a health check carried out with a nurse within two weeks or else I would be deregistered from the GP. It was a long process, but eventually I got to see the doctor. When I was seated in front of the doctor, I was weak, shaking, and restless; I couldn't sit still. The doctor suggested that rather than treating the symptoms, we should treat the root cause since it had been going on for a while. In my mind, I thought, *No way*! At the time, I was so antimedication. The doctor saw that I wasn't ready to go on medication for anxiety, so he prescribed me some antisickness medication. I still asked him to write down the name of anxiety medication he had suggested so I could research it when I got home.

Later I researched the medication, and it put me off. The proportion of the people who had a positive experience using the medication was pretty much the same as the proportion of the people who had a negative experience with the medication. Of course, I know different people can react to the same medication differently. However, for me, who was already against using medication for anxiety at the time, on the particular website I viewed, the reviews were not encouraging based on the proportions of the positive and negative experience.

For my scheduled counselling session for Friday evening, when it was time, I was logged in and was in the "session room" waiting for the counsellor to call me, but she didn't call me and there was no message from her. Eventually, I got impatient and asked to be matched with someone else, which was a feature the app offered. I desperately needed to speak to someone, a professional, someone with whom the whole situation would make sense to, because although I was experiencing it, I couldn't wrap my head around it. That same night, I was matched with someone else. These people were quick, I thought, and I liked them for that already. Not long after that, my new counsellor messaged me to introduce herself and we agreed on a time for our first session, which was the next day, Saturday morning. I had messaged her, asking if it was OK for us to have a voice call instead of a video call, as I was not looking presentable. She said the mode of communication was up to me and however I felt I was looking was fine and didn't matter. I went ahead with the video call, and I am glad I did.

I did not know how I would feel about the first session; it was my first time having proper counselling, although I had gone through a short period of email counselling provided by my university towards the time I was rounding up my modules in Coventry. However, I was glad I was speaking to her. She understood me; she was patient and encouraging. Without interrupting, she listened to me each time I spoke. At the time, I was being laid back and could have done more by getting out of bed, getting something to eat, not being moody and withdrawn, but she encouraged me; she was prepared to work with me. Towards the end of every session, she would always ask me if I had any more questions or concerns. However, during that first session, I said I did not have any questions or concerns, and the next thing she said was, "All right, would you like me to pray us out?" I was surprised but didn't show it. I said yes, and she prayed for me as if she had known me before that time. I instantly liked her.

The Journey to Coventry

The following day, Sunday, I did not feel like it, but I dragged myself to church. I was going to work on Monday, so I might as well go to church. In church, I was weak and couldn't participate much. There was usually a place I liked sitting in church, but that day, I sat at the back. Later that night, as I got ready for work, I knew I was not strong enough to travel to work via public transport, especially because there were quite a few transport changes here and there. I called a few local taxis to find out their prices and then spoke to my mum about my intention. The taxi arrived early in the morning. The journey to work was long, nearly a two-hour ride. When I eventually got to work, I still did not know the suitable drop-off and pick-up location. The driver stopped to drop me off on the opposite side of the road to where I was going. That meant I would have to cross the road and then walk to work. I pleaded with him to drop me on the other side of the road, and he came up with an excuse as to why he couldn't. I just thanked him and got off. As I got out of the taxi and started walking, I did not feel well at all. I was not sure if it was a combination of being weak and sitting in the taxi for so long, but I was uncomfortable. I made it into the building and to the third floor, but I had to sit in reception for a minute, as I was tired. I eventually made it to my desk.

As time went on, my team members noticed I wasn't looking too good, and after asking me some questions, they urged me to go home. It was still quite early; my manager had not even come in. How was I supposed to leave just like that? I appreciated their concern, but I still stayed. When my manager came in, one of the team members looked at me a few times, indicating that I tell my manager I wanted to go home. When they were urging me to go home earlier,

I had said at least let my manager come in first and I can discuss it with him. Eventually, my team member spoke out and said to my manager, "Your staff is not feeling well and does not want to go home." Shortly after, my manager invited me for a chat about what was going on. There are times where you can't tell how genuine someone is or if that person is pretending, but I could see that my manager was genuinely concerned about my health. We agreed that I should go home.

"A man's heart plans his way, But the Lord directs his steps" (Prov. 16:9). As the meeting was coming to an end, my manager asked if he could give me a hug and I said yes. As he hugged me, he told me it was going to be OK. I nearly burst out crying. God really did leave the best for the last. I mentioned earlier on that I would have accepted the first job offer I got due to the stress of my dissertation and because I wanted a job before my course ended. I didn't have to say this aloud at the time, but God knew what was on my mind and heart even better than I did. Of all the interviews I mentioned I attended, only my company permitted teleworking (working from home) when required.

It was also interesting to learn that during my application process, they wanted to hire two people, and even when I joined the company in October 2018, recruitment for the second person was still going on and a second person was not hired until January 2019. One day my manager gave me an estimate of the amount of applications received during my application process. I was beyond shocked. On another occasion, he also said, "We haven't found another Lois." He then laughed. I can't lie; it felt good and my head swelled

The Journey to Coventry

a little. In my mind, I thought, *Wow, come and see the hand of God*. My present manager was one of my interviewers. During our meeting, before deciding I should go home, he had been asking me if the job was stressing me out or was too much. He had started thinking and mentioning ways in which the company could help me. He also told me that if I needed any specific help from the company, I should not hesitate to let him know.

My second interviewer was someone in our team too; he was pretty much in the same position as my manager. If my manager was not available, I could always approach him for help. I let him know what was going on. He told me to take as long as I needed to get better and that I should not worry about work or feel pressured. On one occasion, he told me he was advising me like a daughter that I should never put any job or anything before my health.

What is the essence of mentioning all of this? There is a lesson here that I would like you, my reader, to learn from. On 1 April 2019, I was six months in my company, I didn't know the religion or spiritual beliefs of my manager or my second interviewer. However, one thing is for sure: these people accepted me as part of them from day one. The love and support they showed all through the various challenges was beyond me. Don't get me wrong—various religions teach about love, and I love being taught about love. However, we should not love people, treat people well, show care and support because of a religion but because it is the right thing to do.

Throughout these challenges, it made sense to me why, even when they thought I was fit for the role, they still

Lois T.A. Omorayewa

wanted to know if I was a good fit for the team. They value and care for their team members. I couldn't have asked for a better first job. My manager does not joke when it comes to work and getting things done, yet he is one of the most caring and understanding people I have ever met. He would often go to make tea or something and would ask me if he could get me a drink. In some cultures, in a different part of the world, I would be the one expected to make tea for my manager. When team members were going to buy something, they would often ask if they could get anyone else anything. Everyone got along in the team. There was no unnecessary tension. I love my job. Therefore, be good to others not because you expect anything from others or because you feel pressured but just because it is the right thing to do. It is good to be good.

Back to when I was leaving work that Monday, one of my team members helped me get my laptop from my locker so I could work from home. He went downstairs with me, helped me order my Uber, and walked me to the Uber. The journey was another level of discomfort, but I got home safely. I then decided I needed to speak to my family friend doctor about what had been going on. I didn't want to use medication, but there was no point in going to work like this; I knew it was all anxiety. I wasn't ill, and a blood test confirmed that. I eventually got to speak to him and let him know what was going on. He suggested Propranolol, which is a beta blocker that could help with the anxiety-related symptoms. Furthermore, it was mild and coming off it wouldn't be such a big deal as it could potentially be for some other anxiety medications.

The Journey to Coventry

A few days later, I started using Propranolol. I remember the first day I used it. It was a Saturday. I was so nervous. I had never really been on medications other than one-offs and, in many cases, painkillers. Now here I was, about to go on a medication that calms you down by reducing your heart rate. I prayed on the medication and got my mum to pray on it as well. I took the medication and was in bed for four hours without getting up. I tried to force myself to sleep, but I couldn't. Then, when I eventually tried to get out of bed, I noticed I was calm. Prior to that, there was usually so much adrenaline in the last couple of days that all I needed to do to get a racing heart was to do something as simple as standing up. However, this time around, I was relaxed. Thankfully, the only side effects I experienced for a few days was being a little light-headed, which was possibly due to not eating enough and being on the medication.

On 5 November 2018, a Monday, I was due to have another GP appointment. This time it was a different doctor. Before he was aware that I was on Propranolol, he had suggested another medication but said it could make the anxiety worse in the first three weeks before things started getting better, adding that if it wasn't good enough, I could always try something else. It took a lot in me to accept going on Propranolol. There was no way I was going on a medication that would make the anxiety worse in the first three weeks, nor did I want to experiment with different drugs. I wasn't willing to feel worse than how I was already feeling. Furthermore, that would mean three more weeks of not going to work. *No way!* I thought.

The next day, 6 November 2018, I returned to work but used a taxi. I was still quite anxious about public transport and even sometimes in the taxis. I was still not feeling great but started to feel much better towards the end of the day. My manager and I had agreed that for the time being, I would work from home on Tuesdays and Thursdays, meaning I would be going into the office Mondays, Wednesdays, and Fridays. However, I had told him I would start that the following week since it was already Tuesday and I had been away for a couple of days. I also explained to him that I wanted the opportunity to leave my house as much as possible so I get used to being out again and not surrender to anxiety.

At the close of work that day, I was going to use an Uber home. My second interviewer during the application process walked me downstairs and showed me the best pickup location for the office on the Uber app. He waited with me until the Uber arrived. On the arrival of the Uber, he walked me to the car and asked me if I was feeling anxious. I said no. I was very calm, to my surprise. As I was getting into the Uber, I thanked him. On the way home, I remained calm. I had earphones on, listening to music and relaxing as I watched how well-lit and beautiful London was in the evening after sunset. It had been a long time since I had been in Central London in a car, especially at night. Therefore, through the long drive and traffic, I was observing my environment as much as possible, like a tourist.

When I got home, I was happy. When I got to my room, I knelt and thanked God for the day and me getting to and from work safely, as I had been extremely nervous earlier on in the morning. I then got into the shower, listening to music about God being in control and freedom, and I felt a

The Journey to Coventry

burden being lifted. Afterwards, I ate quite well compared to the last couple of days.

The rest of November was great. I was OK, but the only thing was that I was still scared of taking public transport. I knew I would take it at some point and would be fine. However, I just needed to feel ready to take it and not feel under pressure and take it with someone to get me going again. I was due to go on leave from Thursday, 20 December (working half day) until Thursday, 3 January 2019. My brother was going to be back home before the twentieth. We then planned that, that week, rather than doing my usual working from home on Tuesdays and Thursdays, I would go to work Monday through Wednesday and then work a half day from home on Thursday and then officially be on leave. The plan was that I would go to work on these days with the train and my brother would come with me so that by the time I was resuming in January 2019, I would start taking public transport on my own again.

In December 2018, I was OK. My eating had improved, and I had gained a lot of weight back. As Christmas was approaching, I would make jokes and tell my mum she was cooking all the Christmas food alone and mention everything I wanted her to cook.

Chapter 7

WAS IT REALLY A MERRY CHRISTMAS AND A HAPPY NEW YEAR?

On the evening of Sunday, 17 December 2018, the day I was going to get on the train again since the October 2018 incident on my way home from work, I was getting my things together for work. As I picked out what I was going to wear and packed my bag, I looked at the time and realised I had not yet booked a taxi. I usually prebooked taxis to work the day before and then used Ubers from work back home. I didn't know how I was going to get on the train, but I felt some peace somewhere inside of me. I didn't know what to expect, but at least I would have my brother with me. Eventually, I did book a taxi, but not to work. I booked a taxi to the station a few minutes' drive away, where I usually boarded the train towards the direction of work. I typically needed to get on two buses to get to that station at the time. However, I had lost track of the bus times due to not taking it for quite a while.

The Journey to Coventry

The next morning, we set out for work. I was quite calm; I had prayed my heart out to God the night before, and when I woke up in the morning, I was begging for everything to go well. On the train, I didn't feel any discomfort. My brother kept looking at me, asking if I was OK, but I was fine. Eventually, we were talking, laughing, and taking pictures. At one point, we even called our mum on FaceTime. I took the train to work from Monday through Wednesday that week, as planned. However, I still took Ubers back home on those days. I wanted to ease back into it, especially because the trigger was usually on the way back home. I worked a half day on Thursday as planned, and later that day I was officially on leave.

I didn't know that Friday was going to be the start of yet another battle. "Be sober, be vigilant; because your adversary the devil walks about like a roaring lion, seeking whom he may devour. Resist him, knowing that the same sufferings are experienced by your brotherhood in the world" (1 Pet. 5:8–9 NKJV). I was having McDonald's for dinner and watching a movie. I had finished the chips and was literally on the last bite of the burger when I felt like the food was coming back up instead of going down. I went into a small panic mode. *What is this? I know I said I was going to cut out McDonald's from my diet, but can I just live, please?* I thought. From that point onwards, eating became an issue. The more I ate, the worse it was getting. I googled something about the situation which I can't remember now. I just remembered concluding that I was most likely facing regurgitation based on what I had found on Google. This situation knocked out my appetite in a way I had never experienced. Again, do you now understand that Coventry was never the problem? The more I ate, the more I felt regurgitation sensations, until I stopped eating nearly completely.

The first incident of regurgitation happened on 21 December 2018, just four days before Christmas. Everything I had been trying to build up—more faith, being more prayerful, being more positive, trusting in the process and more—all felt as if it was fading away. "No temptation has overtaken you except such as is common to man; but God is faithful, who will not allow you to be tempted beyond what you are able, but with the temptation will also make the way of escape, that you may be able to bear it" (1 Cor. 10:13 NKJV). It felt as if I were thrown into the deep end of a pool and unable to swim. I was never suicidal, but at that point, I was nearly tired of life. It felt as if each time I was coming out of an anxiety-related challenge, I was walking right into another. I had been so happy earlier on that week due to successfully going to work on the train, and I was looking forward to going back to work using public transport on my own again in January 2019. I kept wondering why this had to happen to me. The few days leading up to Christmas, I was down; I was withdrawn and barely speaking to my family members. I was mostly keeping to myself and crying, and I was already losing weight rapidly. On so many occasions, especially when I couldn't pray the way I would have liked to, I would just tell God that if I had ever taken good health for granted, I was sorry. I was drained and tired and wondered how much longer I would be experiencing all these horrible things.

On Christmas Day, I managed to make a conscious decision to be happy. As I got ready for church, I played different uplifting music aloud and sang along and danced to it. I was

The Journey to Coventry

bubbly and happy. I participated well during the Christmas service. However, on getting back home, I couldn't eat yet again. I could only have two spoons of Jollof rice. The low mood returned. That was all I had on Christmas Day, aside from a few pieces of crackers I had earlier on in the morning before we left for church. Christmas 2018 was on a Tuesday, and for the remaining days of that week, I was mostly in bed doing nothing.

The regurgitation situation was not getting better. On New Year's Eve, I was weak physically and emotionally. I felt unwell and was in bed the entire day. The year of 2018 was far from the best of years for me. I couldn't wait for it to end, yet I was about to go into 2019 feeling less of myself. Usually I looked forward to the New Year's Watch Night Service at church, but I was seriously contemplating whether to go. I eventually decided to attend the service. As I got ready for church and was doing my make-up, I had to take a quick break many times to sit down because of how weak I was. Not too long before we left for church, I held my brother's hand and we agreed in prayer that I would go to church safely, be at church safely, and would return home safely. I prayed I was going to shame the devil.

As we drove to church, I barely said anything in the car. At church, I experienced a series of emotions and physical sensations. I would be feeling uncomfortable, and then the next minute I would be talking to my brother and laughing, and then the next minute, I was angry and moody without a reason. Towards the end of the service, I started to feel much better, both physically and emotionally; I even interacted with a few people at church that night. On the way back home, I was able to talk well and interact with my family, unlike on the way to church earlier on.

The regurgitation situation continued into 2019. It felt that as the days went by, eating become more difficult and unbearable. I was only able to go into the office once, which was the day I was supposed to resume. Other than that, I worked from home for the rest of January 2019 until the end of March 2019 and only resumed back at work on 1 April 2019. The day I mentioned that God spoke to me about what to do because of all that had happened, in which this book is included, was a Sunday. I had planned to go to work the next day in a taxi, with my mum accompanying me. My mum noticed that, that Sunday night, I had been more quiet than usual, but to be honest, I wasn't thinking much of it at the time.

The next morning, as I got ready for work, I knew it wasn't a good idea to go. I was fully dressed, but it took me a lot of sitting down and standing to get dressed, as I was weak. I needed to tell my mum that I didn't think we should go, but I felt bad, as she was already dressed. When she next entered my room, I explained things to her. From her voice and body language, I could tell she was worried. She went to tell my dad. At this point, I had already started crying; I was tired of being tired. My dad and mum both returned to my room to check up on me. There was a minute or so of silence; thinking of it now, I could picture each one of us at that point in time thinking, *What next now?* Shortly after, my dad left and went to call our doctor that we usually contacted. The doctor told my dad to take me to A & E (accident and emergency). I changed into a more

The Journey to Coventry

comfortable outfit, and my mum asked me to pack a few things, thinking I was going to be admitted at the hospital.

Eventually, when we were ready to leave for the hospital, my dad told my mum and I to hang on while he warmed up the car. My mum and I then went to sit in the living room. I suddenly felt a weird cold sensation throughout my body, followed by an overwhelming wave of nausea. I quickly got up and went upstairs to my room to lie down. My mum followed me and asked what had happened. At this point, my dad had warmed up the car and was ready for us to go, but I was pleading for him to give me thirty minutes. Eventually, after the drama of how I was feeling, I was able to make it to the hospital with maximum restlessness. My dad had to push me in a chair that was like a wheelchair.

I had a blood test, and it was all fine. When I eventually got to see a doctor, she wasn't the friendliest doctor. It felt as if she was challenging me rather than trying to help the situation. The doctor told my mum that she could do nothing else and the only other option would be to force-feed me, which meant a tube would be passed through my nose to get nutrients into my body. On that hospital bed, my head was all over the place. I told them to force-feed and do whatever. This was tough on me, and for a moment, I was too numb to care. Whatever wanted to happen should happen, I thought. Eventually, a food disorder specialist was invited. While waiting for her arrival, I had an intravenous drip, as I was very dehydrated. When the eating disorder specialist arrived, she asked me so many questions, including questions about my childhood.

Eventually, she said I should be referred to an eating disorder clinic, but she wouldn't be able to do the referral, as it had to come from my GP. She also recommended that I get an endoscopy, meaning a small camera would have been inserted down my throat to capture the potential cause of any swallowing problems. The woman then said she was going to write a letter to my GP so the process could be speeded up. At my age, the only way I was able to take milk at the hospital that day was using a five-millimetre syringe and gradually releasing it inside one side of my mouth. The eating disorder specialist requested that I be given another drip to give me strength to go home, which I was given. I had some strength in comparison to earlier on in the morning when I got to the hospital. I was eventually discharged and went home with my parents. What a long day it was. "But thanks be to God, who gives us the victory through our Lord Jesus Christ" (1 Cor. 15:57 NKJV).

"'No weapon formed against you shall prosper, and every tongue which rises against you in judgement, you shall condemn. This is the heritage of the servants of the Lord and their righteousness is from me,' says the Lord" (Isa. 54:17 NKJV). The strength did not last more than a day or two, as I was still not eating well. I tried, but it wasn't working out. The strange thing was that I did feel hungry during these periods, but I just couldn't eat. There were times when I would put something in my mouth and subconsciously spit it out instantly. I was on a liquid diet, yet I still found it hard to have my liquid diet reasonably. I could be on half a cup for two hours.

I went back to the cycle of being weak again and was losing more weight by the day. I had gone on a new medication

The Journey to Coventry

a few days before the A & E incident. I continued having GP appointments and my online counselling sessions. At that point, I stopped stressing about work; I liked the job and certainly didn't want to start going through the whole job-hunting experience again, yet my manager had been supportive. If I had lost my job, it would have hurt but it would have been understandable. Not everyone would have been this patient, supportive, and understanding, especially towards a new staff member just coming off probation, and that is fair enough. However, thankfully, I was still given the opportunity to work from home.

I continued trying to figure out what to do about the eating situation with my counsellor; she was getting worried. From when we started to work together, she usually had a habit of praying about issues or concerns before telling me what to do. She was praying about this eating situation, but she was worried, as she was not hearing anything back from God. One day hypnosis dropped into her mind. She also had someone in the same field as she was, and they usually sought each other's opinions in difficult situations. She spoke to the person, and the person suggested hypnosis. When she spoke to me, I was clueless about what to say and thought my parents would not allow that. Even I wasn't sure about how I felt about it. She told me to take my time and think about it, and if I wanted, we could have a session with my mum to explain things to her. She also sent me some videos about it to watch and to also show my mum. My counsellor felt there was a blockage somewhere in my subconscious mind that was making this food issue persist.

I didn't truly consider it initially. However, things were not improving. I didn't like to see the sight of myself in the mirror because of how much weight I had lost. As I write this, I am still on the waiting list of the eating disorder clinic. This couldn't continue; I was looking anorexic and frail to the point that moving around the house was becoming an issue—I was not leaving my house to go anywhere. I seriously started considering this hypnosis. I was reading about it. I had mentioned my counsellor's suggestion to my mum and my brother one day in the middle of a conversation, and their reaction made me think, *OK, never mind*. That was understandable, as I was also sceptical.

Days later, I told my mum that my counsellor wanted her to attend one of my sessions. I mentioned some things that were going to be talked about in the session, but I did not mention hypnotherapy. Eventually, a session was scheduled, and my mum was going to attend. During the session, my counsellor asked my mum about my childhood. My mum gave my counsellor good insight as to how when I was very young, I didn't like eating. She had to force me to eat on many occasions, sometimes bribe me with something and sometimes threaten to smack me. My mum said there were times when she gave me my lunch box for school and I wouldn't even open it to see what was there. I brought it back home untouched.

My mum also mentioned that I didn't like anything to do with vomiting. She further explained how I always wanted to be carried by her as a baby. However, when she was pregnant with my brother, she threw up a lot. She said that whenever she was throwing up, I would cry and run away from her. I would then stand at a distance and say mummy sorry, and after that, for the next hour or two, I wouldn't let her carry me. Maybe that blockage that my

The Journey to Coventry

counsellor talked about was the fear of throwing up. My subconscious had probably associated throwing up with danger, even though consciously I never thought throwing up would harm me.

Growing up, I knew that was a phobia I had, but it never really affected me. I just didn't like the concept of it. I enjoyed eating out and had a sweet tooth. My counsellor then spoke to my mum about hypnotherapy, and my mum asked many questions. Eventually, my mum spent a few days studying hypnotherapy and watching videos about how it was carried out after which she was now the one explaining somethings about it to me and telling me it was not dangerous, as we had thought. I agreed with my family to have a session done for me. I then started looking for Christian hypnotherapists, but they were hard to find. Eventually, I just started looking for a normal hypnotherapist. I called a few here and there; I then came across the website of a psychotherapist who had many years of experience. He had many qualifications and accreditations related to psychology and mental health. I also read that he trained doctors, nurses, psychologists, and psychotherapists. I sent his website link to my counsellor to let me know what she thought of it. She got back to me and said she was happy with what she saw. She wanted me to go ahead with him.

I got in contact with his office, which then led to a phone consultation, and a home appointment was booked for the following week. The appointment was on a Monday. My dad and brother were home (a requirement from the hypnotherapist was that someone needed to be at home with me during the session). Prior to the session, we had prayed as a family that God would make a way through this session. When he eventually arrived, I was nervous, as I didn't know how I would feel in the process or the impact the session would have on me. However, this man was good and knew what he was doing. Another lesson to learn here is not to judge a book by its cover. Prior to my counsellor suggesting hypnotherapy, I had a misconception about it. Of course, different people can have varying experience depending on the psychotherapist/hypnotherapist.

During the first session, I sat on the couch in my living room, my eyes closed. I had been instructed to breathe in and out for a few moments. I was fully conscious, but this time around, we were dealing with my subconscious. There were a series of things the man said that I can't remember now. However, one of the effective exercises he made me do while still in that position was to imagine myself with a baggage of all these problems; I didn't want, walking across a bridge over a river and throwing all these problems one after the other. He didn't rush me. He gave me time to do it at my pace and give him a thumbs up when I was ready to proceed. Although I was seated in the living room, it felt as if I was actually throwing my problems away. Behind where he was seated in the living room, there was a big portrait of me from my BSc graduation. I had told him I wanted to gain weight and wanted to go back to the office. He looked at the picture and told me to look at it, saying I could be like that again. He said I would be able to go to work again. He also got me to imagine (with my eyes closed and still in the relaxed stage) eating my favourite food and enjoying it and the food nourishing me.

The Journey to Coventry

When the session ended, he assured us that I was going to be fine, that he had dealt with worse cases than this and the outcome was positive. He also told me I should start eating whatever I wanted or felt like but also suggested that places like McDonald's and other similar fast foods were not ideal, especially due to the way they were preserved. I was wearing a rope during the first session, and he told me that when I wake up everyday, I should get dressed as if I were going to work and sit at my desk while I was still working from home. Later that day, I had Nando's; at some point, as I was eating, I was crying. From not being able to eat even bread or crackers, which were things I usually relied on when I couldn't eat, I was now eating truly solid food; it was overwhelming. I continued to eat gradually that week. I had not touched any of the liquid things I used to have.

Then came another big blow. Thursday night I was in a little discomfort. I was constipated and decided to go to bed. I couldn't sleep; I kept tossing around. I was in constant pain. The entire night, I had only forty minutes of sleep before I continued tossing and turning into the morning. I had searched for what medication I could use, and early in the morning, my dad went to buy it for me. I didn't know if the medication was working, but I was just in pain. I nearly slipped back into the pattern of not eating. Moving was difficult, as was eating. I could be chewing or drinking something and the pain would come. I don't know what exactly it feels like to be pregnant, but it felt like contractions. I would suddenly feel intense pain, which sometimes caused me to bang on the wall with my hands a few times or hold my pillow as if I were about to rip it off; sometimes I was holding on to my bed.

The constipation lasted for a week; it was not a happy week. Many times, the contraction-like feeling woke me up several times in one night; that was how painful it was. Sleeping became an extreme sport, quite difficult. Then my miracle came! The constipation pain started to ease off a bit, and then I gradually started eating again. My GP had prescribed another medication to help with the constipation. Funnily enough, the day the medication arrived was the same day the constipation stopped, without my taking the medication, and from that point going forward, I started to eat as if I were being introduced to food. I gradually started gaining weight (I had lost approximately twenty four kilograms during this period of the eating difficulties), and I had fully regained my strength.

I had two more sessions with the hypnotherapist. The second session was during the week I was constipated. I had similar exercises to the first session. One of the exercises was being relaxed and imagining myself picking out old leaves that represented various problems and then burning them, then going to a healthy tree and picking up leaves that represented things I wanted, such as good health, faith, peace, courage, boldness, and restoration.

I had a final session with the hypnotherapist a week after that. We talked about resuming going to church and then eventually work. I had not been going anywhere. The psychotherapist asked me how I liked to dress up to go to church and work, and I told him. For both church and work individually, he got me to close my eyes while being relaxed and imagining myself dressed how I liked to for each location and then imagine myself taking the entire journey to church and back, and I also did the same with

The Journey to Coventry

going to work and back. After that, we took a short walk. That was the first time I took a walk in a couple of weeks.

I have now fully gone back to work. I now walk down the route that used to cause me panic attacks both on my way to work and back without any triggers. I now find it more difficult working from home and prefer being in the office. I now take public transport on my own and go wherever I want. I have an increased appetite and eat whatever I want. I have gained my twenty four kilograms back and I am now watching my weight! LOL! I am now full of strength, I no longer get tired easily and I now work out in the gym. I am now happier than I ever remember being. Life feels great again!

I am still a work in progress.

"She is clothed with strength and dignity, and she laughs without fear of the future" (Prov. 31:23 NKJV).

She is Lois Omorayewa.

Chapter 8
LESSONS LEARNED AND TAKEAWAY

- **Acceptance:** In my opinion, before you can seek solution to an issue or challenge, you should have identified and accepted that the issue or challenge is there. Initially, I refused to accept that I was experiencing anxiety, especially because I was usually fit and healthy, yet anxiety usually had a way of nearly knocking me out completely physically. Acceptance does not mean you are further welcoming what the issue or challenge may be—in this case, mental health. Nor does it mean you are surrendering to and accepting to be defeated by the situation. Instead, view it as a way of identifying what the issue is to guide you into making the right decision to move forward.

- **Identify your triggers:** In the case of mental health challenges, it is important to identify triggers. In my experience, it is one of the most effective way to push you towards the direction of getting the right support that you need for whatever the nature of your situation is. Everyone is different, and different people may have

The Journey to Coventry

different triggers. Two people can respond to the same triggers differently.

- **Seek help:** I can't explain how much I wish I had sought help earlier. Thankfully, people are talking about mental health more now than back in the ancient days. However, there is still a lot more to be done in terms of creating more awareness and seeking help. People are suffering in silence! People are scared to ask for help due to the possibility of being judged or stigmatized. Please look after your mental health as much as you would look after your physical health. Seek help! There is nothing wrong with counselling; there is nothing wrong with using medication; and very importantly, there is nothing wrong with *you*. It is a challenge. Yes, easier said than done, but life is full of challenges and approaches us in different shapes and forms.

- **Resilience:** I am not going to sugar-coat things, but hard work and resilience are required. It might not always be easy, but that's OK. As excited as a student might be to progress to university to bag a degree, it wouldn't necessarily always be an enjoyable journey for the entire duration. You would have to work for your grades to earn that degree. In the same way, you have to be prepared to defeat and not to be defeated. It may not always be easy, but as I have said a few times in this book, when we fall, we rise. If you fall, get up! Don't stay down, because that is not where you belong.

- **Support systems and coping mechanisms:** It is important that you have a support system of people you can always turn to on "one of those days". It does not have to be many people; I was blessed with a group of people that always made themselves available for me, either physically or virtually. Sometimes just talking about how I felt made me feel a bit better. I felt worse when I was keeping to myself, being withdrawn, and not wanting to talk to anyone. You must not allow whatever challenge you experience defeat you.

Coping mechanisms are also important. My coping mechanisms were prayer, the word of God, gospel and inspirational music, listening to uplifting sermons, mindfulness, meditation, watching movies, online shopping and buying things I like, as well as working from home. Yes, working from home was a coping mechanism for me. It kept me occupied rather than being idle for weeks. Being able to attend my Skype meetings from home and work from home made me feel useful, even though there were times where I felt I could be adding much more to the business had all these challenges not occurred. Again, everybody is different. We all have varying coping mechanisms.

One way of having easy access to your coping mechanism, which my counsellor recently told me about, is having a coping mechanism box with anything you like that would help you in the time of stress. For me, based on some of my coping mechanisms I have listed above, my coping mechanism box consists of many sticky notes with Bible verses and spare earphones to remind me about my inspirational and gospel music. I have positive quotes and affirmations in it, and I have the words *breathe* and *relax* in it. I also have the BIH Foundation's logo in it because I want to remember that it is no longer all about me. Instead, I have found a new purpose in helping and reassuring people that mental health challenges do not have to make them feel like the living dead, as it once made me feel.

- **Positive thinking, speaking, and affirmations:** It is difficult to entertain negative thoughts and speak positively. You may not always be able to control the presence and frequency of negative thoughts. When these thoughts come, don't fight them; allow them to come and then counter them with positive speaking and affirmations and move on. You don't have to speak exactly what you feel; look at yourself in the mirror and tell yourself what you would like to feel like. Keep speaking positively until positivity becomes a part of you and you start believing those words, and even then, keep speaking positively. There are many times I look at myself in the mirror and affirm myself. There are also many times when I'm talking to myself in second person, calling my name and using the word *you* to represent myself and speaking over myself, my health, my present, and my future.

- **Be patient:** One thing about me in the early stages of my challenge with anxiety is that I was always in a rush to get better; even my counsellor had noticed this. This often led to me putting unnecessary pressure on myself and setting unrealistic recovery goals. Whatever you can't control, let go; don't force it. Be patient and trust in the process. Be patient with yourself, be patient with your surroundings, do what you have to do, and leave the rest to God. When I started writing this book, I had nothing planned other than the book title. I didn't know how I was going to organise it or what the chapter names would be. I just prayed each time before I started writing and asked God that his will alone be done, and I just moved with the flow. This is my story, but it is not about me. It's about whoever can pull strength and encouragement from my experience.

- **Take baby steps and run your own race:** Everyone is different and unique in their own way. Everyone has different strengths, different capabilities, different breaking points, and so on. There were times where I knew of other people who were coping fine with anxiety, and I would wonder why my case was so different, but now I know better. Never compare yourself with another person. Everyone has their own challenges to deal with. Different people are built for different challenges, and I believe that is one of the beauties of diversity. Run your own race; courage is not pretending to have it all together. Courage is taking baby steps, not downsizing the progress made from the baby steps, and continuing on.

- **Show love to all:** Permit me to bring religious institutions into this. When I first started researching and learning more about anxiety and mental health in general, I found stories of people online whereby they had mental health challenges, but their various religious institutions were the last place they wanted to be in or seek help. Why? Because they felt judged and uncomfortable. Mental health does not mean you don't have faith—the same way you can have faith but still fall ill or need medication. Mental health is not

The Journey to Coventry

a respecter of people, and it can happen to anyone. Don't get me wrong: even if you suffer from a mental health challenge, you can't just play victim and indulge in self-pity; that is not going to get you anywhere. There are scriptures in the Bible like the likes of the kingdom of God suffering violence but the violence taketh it by force. However, we need to know where to draw the line. We live in an uncompassionate era. People don't want to reach out to people they are not familiar with, and I am guilty of this. We live in an era where rather than asking if someone is OK and how we can help—thinking *this person doesn't look too good, let me have a chat with him or her*, and so on—instead, we don't care. We walk past people without noticing them; we take pride in spreading information about the unfortunate things people go through. There have been many situations where I was well dressed and well made up, yet you would never think anything was wrong. However, I was anxious, low in mood, and so on.

My beloved reader, someone within your reach may need you more than you can ever imagine. Love people, care for people, and help people whenever you can.

The Bring It Home Foundation (BIH)
(www.bihfoundation.com)

The Bring It Home Foundation (BIH), as I mentioned at the start of this book, is a foundation that is set up to create more awareness about mental health, specifically anxiety and depression, and support people with these challenges in my country of origin, Nigeria. I am acting based on what God spoke to me and laid upon my heart. Therefore, I can't promise expansion of any sort now. However, if you or anybody you know has any anxiety-related or depression-related challenges, please drop us an email at info@bihfoundation.co.uk. Please don't hesitate, irrespective of whatever country or region you are in, and we can evaluate how we can support you. Even if you need to just talk to someone in full confidentiality, we are here for you.

As part of this project, we also have a YouTube channel called the BIH Foundation, which features content such as our activities from our awareness campaigns and talk shows, sometimes including featured mental health professionals and Q&A sessions. Feel free to subscribe and watch that space.

Conclusion

In conclusion, I would like to thank you, my beloved reader, for taking time out to read this book. Being this open with you in this book was not an easy decision for me to make. However, even if it inspires and helps just a few people, it was worth it. Whether you are experiencing mental health challenges or not, I hope you have been blessed and inspired by this book. I hope you have at least gained one or two things to take away from here. Feel free to reach out to us via the email address above for further enquires. Remain blessed.

Lightning Source UK Ltd.
Milton Keynes UK
UKHW012103010719
345380UK00001B/19/P